BOOTS AND BREWS

BOOTS & BREWS

walking, food and folklore around Morecambe Bay

BETH & STEVE PIPE

First published in 2019
by Palatine Books,
Carnegie House,
Chatsworth Road
Lancaster LA1 4SL
www.palatinebooks.com

British Library Cataloguing-in-Publication data
A catalogue record for this book is available from the British Library

Paperback ISBN 13: 978-1-910837-23-8

Designed and typeset by Carnegie Book Production
www.carnegiebookproduction.com

Printed and bound by Cambrian Press

Grange-over-Sands
Arnside
Ulverston
Cark
Birkrigg
Carnforth
Walney Island
Hest Bank
Morecambe
Heysham
Glasson Dock
Knott End
Morecambe Bay

Introduction

Welcome to *Boots & Brews: walking, food and folklore around Morecambe Bay* – the name says it all really! This book is chock full of fabulous walks around Morecambe Bay and all of them come with a pub, a café, and/or somewhere to buy a sarnie or a pie before (or after) you set out. We've even given away our favourite picnic spots on each route so you know when to break into your packed lunch, because there is nothing more infuriating on a walk than tucking into your sandwiches, perched on an inhospitable rock, only to find the perfect place a few hundred yards (or metres) further on.

Each walk also comes with an escape route for those folks who don't fancy the whole hike (though none of them is long), as well as three different satellite strolls if you want to explore the area a little bit more. We haven't provided specific directions to these, but they are all easy to find on a map.

We've also dug into a little bit of the local history, but if, like me, you hated history lessons at school then please don't panic because we've tried to keep our historical nuggets short, sharp, interesting and occasionally funny.

As ever, we've tried to make the directions as accurate as possible but please do always take some form of back up with you; if you're using your mobile, apps such as ViewRanger are free to download, come with a range of free maps and should be able to locate where you are at any given point on the routes. And there are always good old fashioned paper maps too, of course. None of these walks really heads out into the wilds but it's always worth ensuring you are properly kitted out with waterproof shoes and clothing, just in case.

We absolutely love Morecambe Bay and consider ourselves incredibly fortunate to live here. We really hope our love for the area, its history, wildlife and (of course) food comes through in this book and inspires you to linger a little longer, explore a little further and eat a little more. I promise you'll never be disappointed.

Table of Walks

Pilling Windmill

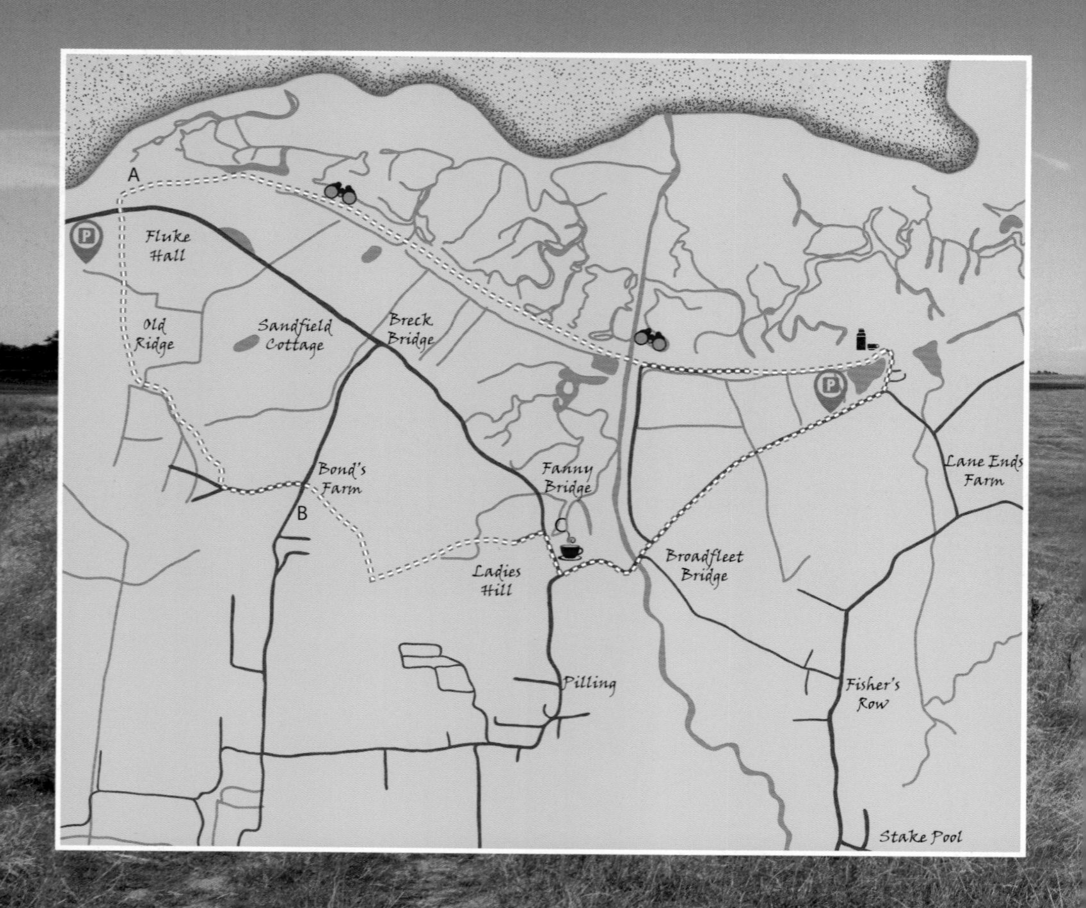
A
Fluke Hall
Old Ridge
Sandfield Cottage
Breck Bridge
Bond's Farm
B
Fanny Bridge
C
Ladies Hill
Broadfleet Bridge
Lane Ends Farm
Pilling
Fisher's Row
Stake Pool

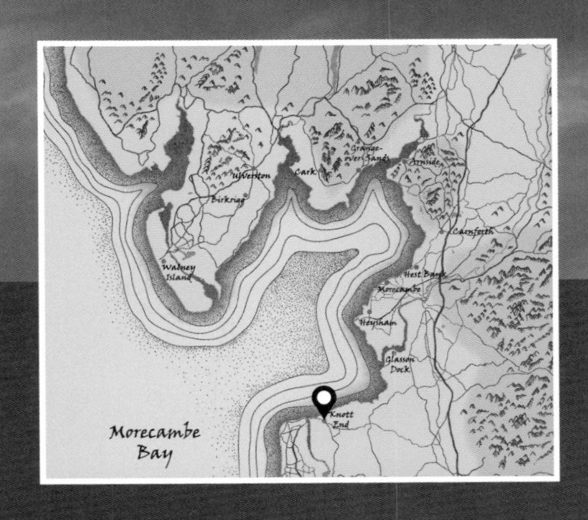

Knott End

Route details

Start: Pilling Amenity Area car park

Grid Ref: SD 41504 49473

Distance: 4.0 miles/6.4km

Terrain: Hard track, salt marsh, tarmac, fields

Difficulty: A flat route with some navigation required. **PLEASE NOTE: This walk is NOT accessible between 26th December and Good Friday due to ground nesting birds, and dogs are not allowed on the embankment at any time**

Parking: Free car park at Pilling Amenity Area

Public transport: Local buses

Facilities: Golden Ball Pub, Pilling – a popular local Thwaites pub, especially cosy in the autumn/winter months

Best picnic spot: Right at the start/end of the walk

Route

From the car park head up onto the embankment and turn left towards a gate. Pass through the gate and continue following the embankment all the way around the headland. When you reach a fence drop down to the right to the salt marsh, to cross the field boundary and continue following the coast around until you reach a concrete slipway **(Point A)**. Turn left here, cross a small car park and follow the public footpath leading off through the field opposite.

Continue on until you reach the remains of two houses on a small hill. Cross the stile to reach the houses and follow the waymarked route between them. In the field beyond head for the far right-hand corner and use the enclosed footbridge to reach the field. Keep to the left-hand field boundary, cross another bridge on your left and turn hard right. Cross another stile and bear diagonally left across the field to reach a small bridge stile leading to houses; continue past the houses then turn left to reach the tarmac lane (**Point B**).

At the lane turn right then almost immediately left through the yard of the white house to reach the small gate beyond. Go through the gate; bear diagonally right across the field to reach the stile on the far corner next to a metal gate. Cross the stile and continue on, keeping the field boundary on your left. Before you reach the end of the large field take the stile leading left and follow the footpath towards the church and village. Cross another stile to reach a hard track and continue on to the road (**Point C**).

Turn right along the road, then left at the T-junction next to the pub. Remain on this road as it passes through the village, then keep left after the bridge to follow Black Sands Lane back to the car park.

ESCAPE ROUTE: At **Point A** turn left along the road and follow it to **Point C** (3.5 miles)

About the walk

I'll be honest, when I was researching this chapter I came across a post in a forum on the internet asking, "Is it true that there's absolutely nothing to see or do in Knott End?" They're not the words that a researcher likes to be met with when trying to dig out interesting facts and historical details for a book. I guess it all really rather depends on what you enjoy seeing and doing. For example, I know people who tell me that there's nothing to see or do in Blackpool because it doesn't appeal to them; these are possibly the people who would find a trip to Knott End interesting and enjoyable.

The embankment, which forms the first section of the walk, was created in 1981 by the North West Water Authority (now United Utilities). It was built to protect the nearby farmland and villages from flooding following a particularly severe storm on 11th November 1977, when over 5000 homes and nearly 8000 acres of agricultural land were flooded. The area is now a haven for wildlife, which is why dogs are barred completely and access for everyone is restricted during the nesting and migration season. On our short walks there we've easily spotted curlews, knotts and egrets, and the area is popular with serious birdwatchers who have spotted many rare and interesting species, particularly during the migration season.

One of the most prominent claims to fame for the village is its Viking links. The Vikings came to Lancashire from Dublin in the 10th century, and although they have a historical reputation for violence the reality is that many of them were simply traders. Their legendary boating prowess meant they often approached new areas from the sea and built their trading routes from there. Due to the fact that this all happened so long ago much of what is said to be fact is, in reality, folklore, but it makes for an interesting story. Apparently a Viking by the name of Haakon (or Haken) arrived in the area and either laid siege to the area with raping and pillaging, or came in peace to live a quiet life, depending on which story you believe. His remains are buried under Haakon's Mound in nearby Preesall and the mound has since become the site of the local war memorial.

Given the formation of the estuary it's likely that the area offered a suitably safe place to moor and shelter boats, although the sands in the estuary will have shifted considerably over the intervening centuries. The large area of sands alongside the walk are known as Bernard Wharf and are said to have been named after St Bernard, a twelfth-century French abbot who, as well as founding the Cistercian order, is, apparently, the patron saint of skiing, snowboarding, hiking, backpacking and mountaineering. He was certainly a man who loved the outdoors and once said "Believe me, for I know, you will find something far greater in the woods than in books. Stones and trees will teach you that which you cannot learn from the masters." So it seems appropriate to have such a beautiful and atmospheric area named after him.

Another famous name associated with the area is the artist L.S. Lowry, who painted the jetty at Knott End (not in a twenty-tins-of-outdoor-emulsion-from-B&Q kind of way, more in a pastel-on-canvas kind of way). He had a long association with the area, having spent family holidays there when he was younger and then returning over the years as he developed his skills as an artist. Although primarily known for painting industrial landscapes he regularly visited the region to sketch and paint the seascapes and coastlines around the Fylde. There is a striking sculpture of him on the seafront at Knott End, not far from the ferry, where he was known to pause and sketch.

While we're on the subject of the ferry, it began service in the 1830s but it had a far from smooth start in life, with ownership and

St John the Baptist Church Pilling

The Embankment, Pilling

operation of the ferries going back and forth between a number of parties throughout its formative years. Several boats have fulfilled the role of ferry and the route has waxed and waned in popularity, as it is challenging to run it commercially all year around. For a time it only ran during the summer months but now there is a year-round service operated by Lancashire County Council and Wyre Borough Council, providing a much-needed service for the local population.

As you pass through Pilling towards the end of the walk you'll not be able to miss Pilling Windmill; although now lacking its sails it is still a striking building. It was originally constructed by Ralph Slater in 1808 to replace a wooden mill which had previously stood there, and it was converted to steam power in 1886, shortly after which the sails were removed. It was operational through until 1926 but then fell into disrepair before being rescued, renovated and converted into a private home. When it was originally built it was the tallest mill in the Fylde but sometime after it was converted to steam the top was removed, most likely due to storm damage, thus reducing its height. In 2007 the then owners worked with a traditional millwright to fit a 'Lancashire boat cap' to the mill, thus making it the tallest mill on the Fylde once again.

Satellite strolls

Fleetwood

Fleetwood was once a popular holiday destination and there are some lovely long walks along the seafront which will remind you of how it was in its heyday. The views out to the Lake District fells are spectacular and the vast expanses of sand are popular with horse riders and water sports enthusiasts.

Knott End

There are some interesting walks along the estuary from Knott End and several paths that loop in through Preesall, where you'll find the remains of an old salt mine and old railway line, the latter providing a nice flat stroll with lovely views down towards Blackpool.

Blackpool

Not everyone's cup of tea, I know, but a great place for a seafront walk with something to keep most people happy. The broad flat prom means it's perfect for folks with mobility issues and the Comedy Carpet in front of the tower is bound to make you chuckle. During the autumn months there are also spectacular murmurations around the piers, which you can enjoy before you take a stroll along the illuminations.

Glasson Dock
Glasson Marsh
Old Glasson
Glasson Dock
Chapel Hill
Kendal Hill
Abbey Lighthouse Cottage
Tomlinson's Farm
Clarkson's Farm
Thurnham Moss
Gardener's Farm
Lancashire Coastal Way
Thursland Hill
A
B
C
D

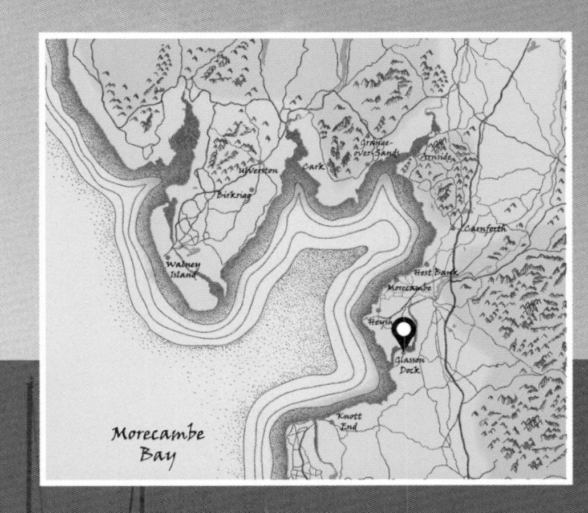

Glasson Dock

Route details

Start: Glasson Dock car park

Grid Ref: SD 44613 56089

Distance: 5.0 miles/8km

Terrain: Tarmac, hard track, grass

Difficulty & duration: A longer route but all flat

Parking: Large pay & display car park at Glasson Dock

Public transport: Local buses

Facilities: There are two pubs plus a café and burger van in Glasson dock which are open throughout the year

Our top picks: The Dalton Arms – a Thwaites pub with a warm welcome and great menu. Lantern O'er Lune – friendly café with dockside views and a seasonal menu

Best picnic spot: Cockersands Abbey

Overlooking Plover Scar Lighthouse

Route

From the car park head out onto the road; turn left, then left again over the swing bridge. Follow the road uphill to a T-junction with an information point and turn left. Follow the road as it drops downhill slightly then take Marsh Lane on your right (**Point A**). Follow the track past the caravan park and through 2 gates onto farmland. Keep to the right-hand field boundary then swing left to pass through a metal gate and over a small bridge. Remain on the farm track until you emerge on the coast.

Turn left and follow the Lancashire Coastal Way, past the Lighthouse Cottage (**Point B**), all the way around to Cockersands Abbey. From the Abbey take the track leading away from the coast, through the farm buildings and remain on the track down to the tarmac lane. Turn left along the lane, keeping right at the fork (**Point C**), and continue on, passing a number of small farms until you reach the signed lane (Jeremy Lane, **Point D**) for Glasson Dock on your left. Follow this lane down to the canal bridge then turn left from the bridge to drop down to the towpath and return to the car park.

ESCAPE ROUTE 1: At **Point B** at the lighthouse just prior to Cockersands Abbey, turn left to follow Slack Lane then Moss Lane to **Point C** (4 miles).

ESCAPE ROUTE 2: From **Point A** remain on the road and follow it around to rejoin the main route at Brow's Bridge (1 mile).

About the walk

For such a relatively short walk this one really packs in a lot of history, and it starts with the docks themselves. Before they were built Glasson was known as Old Glasson and was little more than a small collection of farms and fishing cottages. But, within the space of a few years, it became one of the largest and busiest ports in the North West.

The original docks were built in 1779 and expanded in 1787 to enable them to house 25 merchant ships. Originally cargos would have been moved to Lancaster either by road or, once the link to the Lancaster canal was built in 1826, along the canal, but when the railways arrived in the late 1800s they took over that role. Sadly the line closed to passengers in the 1930s and was then closed completely in 1964. However, the old line is still used as a popular cycle route and forms the start (or end, depending on which way you're going) of the Morecambe Bay Cycleway (Sustrans Route 700).

Near the start of the walk you'll pass a street on your right named Ten Row. This name intrigued me as it's often the case that unusual street names have some historical connection, and in this case the name dates back to the growth and evolution of the port. When the port was originally built there was no need for additional housing

Glasson Dock lock

Lancaster Canal

as the boats arriving were pretty much self-contained, but as the port grew and the link to the Lancaster Canal was established, there became a need to house the workers and labourers. A number of houses were built in the mid 1800s and although many of them still remain, in many cases the names have changed. Ten Row is a row of ten houses built around 1841 and the only one in the village to retain its name. If you take a wander along the short street you'll notice that the houses are much simpler than the ones on the main road, and that's because the ones on the main road belonged to two of the owners of the shipyard.

I'm really quite fond of the viewpoint at the top of Tithebarn Hill as, on a clear day, it gives a real feel for the geography of the area – the information board there is really useful, but try and imagine what it might have been like before any of the buildings were there. The large expanses of marshland all around Morecambe Bay give the area a unique atmosphere and have inspired plenty of poets and painters over the years, as well as being home to a vast array of wildlife. The likes of J.M.W. Turner were inspired by the huge skies above the bay, and it's one of Europe's most important habitats for migrating birds.

As you arrive at the coast one of the first things you'll spot is Plover Scar lighthouse, a place with an interesting recent history. It was built in 1847 as the lower of two leading lights – the second, or high, light was at Lighthouse Cottage, which you'll pass as you walk around the coast. Plover Scar guided thousands of vessels over its many years of service, but on the night of 5th March 2016 it was badly damaged by an empty cargo vessel on its way into Glasson Dock. In September that year phase 1 of a complete refurbishment began with a brick by brick deconstruction of the lighthouse. All the bricks were laid out so they could be replaced in their exact original position and the dome was sent away to be worked on separately.

It was no mean feat as the contractors (MPM North West Ltd, Maryport) could only work at low tide. By January 2017 the deconstruction was completed so the rebuilding could begin, and in May 2017 the lighthouse was fully returned to its former glory. If you're visiting at high tide it's hard to imagine that the lighthouse is just a relatively short scramble across the rocky shore when the tide is out.

The main building of historical interest in the area is Cockersand Abbey and even though only a small part of it remains, it's still an interesting and impressive structure. Some people have described its position as 'bleak' but I think that's a little harsh; it's definitely wild and windswept out on the headland, but it's also incredibly beautiful. The abbey began life in 1180 as a hermitage before becoming a hospital for lepers; by 1190 it had become a priory and in 1192 it was designated a abbey. Sadly it was dissolved by Henry VIII in 1539.

The only part of the abbey remaining intact is the Chapter House which, when looked at from a short distance, has a shape reminiscent of a medieval helmet. There are also the remains of a number of walls but a full and detailed excavation has yet to be carried out. It's thought that some of the stones from the abbey were used in the construction of the nearby farmhouse, as was the custom of the time (an early form of recycling!). It also makes an excellent windbreak if you're looking for somewhere to have your lunch on a blustery day.

The very last part of the walk follows the link to the Lancaster Canal – and I do like a nice canal. When they were built, canal builders were required by law to provide access across their canals for farmers etc., which explains why there are more bridges over canals then there are over rivers. The numbering of the bridges was a navigational aid (and very handy when writing walking guides too!) but the mile markers always confuse me as they appear the wrong way around – if you look closely at them they tell you how far you've come, rather than how far you have to go. This is because they were used to calculate tolls for carrying cargo along the canal, and both the boatmen and the canal owners needed to calculate how far the boat had travelled in order to levy the correct toll.

Cockersands Abbey

Plover Scar Lighthouse

One last stopping off point before you return to the start point is Christ Church, built in 1839–40 and designed by Lancaster architect Edmund Sharpe. It is a small but very lovely church with a well-tended graveyard and a good array of wild flowers in the summer months.

Satellite strolls

Morecambe Bay Cycle Way

Not so much a walk as a rather long bike ride, but definitely worth the effort. The Morecambe Bay Cycleway opened in June 2016 and stretches all the way from Glasson Dock in the south to Sandy Gap on Walney Island in the north (not far from the starting point of the Walney Island walk in this book). Large sections of it are off road and the rest follows quiet country lanes with very few nasty hills and plenty of places for a brew and a view.

Coastal Footpath

From Glasson the coastal footpath stretches off in both directions and is interesting and enjoyable to follow. We were conscious that we needed to keep all the walks in this book below 5 miles, but if you fancy extending your route then grab an OS Map, continue on further around the coast, and loop back down to Glasson a little further along.

Sambo's Grave

Just to the south of this walk, near to Sunderland Point, is a reminder of the region's involvement in the slave trade. Sambo's Grave marks the final resting place of a young black slave who arrived in the region with his master around 1736. Sadly he was taken ill, died and was buried in an unmarked grave, but in 1795 James Watson, a retired head teacher, raised funds to erect a memorial and wrote the poem on the plaque.

B
Sandylands
Fanny House Farm
Lower Heysham
C
Heysham Head
A
Heysham
Higher Heysham
Heysham Moss
Half Moon Bay

Heysham

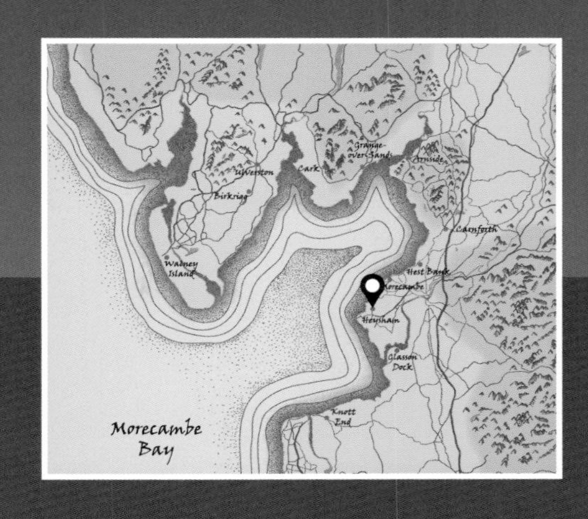

Route details

Start: Half Moon Bay car park

Grid Ref: SD 40846 60790

Distance: 4.5 miles/7.2km

Terrain: Tarmac, hard track

Difficulty: A straightforward route with spectacular views

Parking: Free car park at Half Moon Bay

Public transport: Local buses

Facilities: Café at start/end of walk plus a number of cafés and an excellent pub along the route

Our top picks: Half Moon Bay Café – a small, unassuming but friendly café with superb views across the bay. The Royal in Heysham village – good selection of food and beers

Best picnic spot: LOTS to choose from – anywhere on the benches along the prom, or on the beach near the start

Overview

A 'there and back' route isn't everyone's first choice but the different elevations offer varied routes along the bay and to the churches, plus there are some hidden views which can only be seen properly from the higher road above the prom.

Route

From the car park walk towards the shore, cross the road and follow the waymarked footpath leading diagonally up across the field. Remain on this path until it reaches the road then turn left and follow the road to Heysham village. Cross the road where it bears right and turn left along Bailey Lane (**Point A**). Continue ahead as the road becomes Knowlys Road and climbs slightly. At the top of the hill take the signed footpath to the shore on the left, once you reach the shore turn right along the promenade. As you near the second large stone water break turn right to follow a red tarmac road up to a row of houses then turn left to follow the road above the prom. Continue straight on along this road until it drops down to join another road, turn left here to reach the prom then right along the prom and bear left to reach the end of the large stone jetty (**Point B**).

From the jetty return along the prom towards Heysham, keeping to the lower path, and follow it all the way to the end. Climb the stone steps and continue on, past a small café, to the road (**Point C**). Turn right along the road then follow it around to the left until you reach the churches on your right. Turn right here and follow the footpath past the churches and out onto the clifftops. Go straight on through the gate and follow the path all the way back to Heysham. Once you reach the starting point bear right to walk along the road to Near Naze lighthouse then retrace your steps back to the starting point.

ESCAPE ROUTE: When you first reach the prom turn left to reach **Point C** and follow the main route from there (1.5 miles).

About the walk

These days Heysham is perhaps best known for its power station or ferry port, but there has been a settlement here since at least 1066. It was mentioned in the Doomsday Book (1086) and the ruins of St Patrick's church on the headland are thought to date back to the 8th century, but I'm getting ahead of myself...

You arrive in the village via Barrows Lane alongside a lovely open park. Just along the road to your left is the Heritage Centre (situated in an ancient barn) which is definitely worth visiting to learn more about the history of the village. Along here you'll also find an unassuming small cottage which was once the centre of a bustling local enterprise, as it is where Granny Burrows used to brew her famous Nettle Beer, made from local herbs and nettles with added sugar, yeast and lemons. It sold for 3d a glass (the equivalent of around 40p today) and it was claimed to have restorative properties, including hair regrowth and helping those with rheumatism.

Our walk route then takes you past Heysham Jubilee Institute, built in 1897 and still the village hub, with regular meetings and social

St Peter's Church, Heysham

Near Naze Lighthouse

events. At the end of Bailey Lane, just after you bear right, is where the village water pump used to stand, right in the middle of the road, until it was (unsurprisingly) hit by a car in the 1930s.

Just before you turn left to follow the small lane to the prom pause for a moment, look out to sea, and enjoy Turner's view. When the artist visited here in 1816 he made four pencil sketches from somewhere near this spot which he then used as the basis for his famous watercolour 'Heysham and Cumberland Mountains'. As was the fashion it was somewhat romanticised, but you can still easily pick out the main geographical features.

Over recent years a substantial amount of money has been invested in the promenade, which runs from here all the way around the coast to Hest Bank, and it's a hive of activity, popular with runners, cyclists and walkers. It's perfect for those with mobility issues and the whole way along there are interesting features and nuggets of local information. Look out for the plaques set into the floor to learn a lot of fascinating facts about the area. The higher route out above the prom gives you the opportunity to admire some of the more artistic features from above.

Tombs at St Patrick's church, Heysham

When you return back to the village, along the road just after the small café look out for the little lane on your right leading down to the shore; this is Lade End and is where locals would top up their incomes by collecting mussels from the rocky outcrops around the bay. The horses and carts would come and go from Lade End, taking the mussels from the shore into Morecambe town, from where they would be sent down to London. The practice continued through into the early 1900s and the rocky outcrops are still clearly visible.

Just before you turn up the lane towards the churches, look for St Patrick's well set into the wall on the left. It is one of two holy wells in the town but the only one still surviving, albeit only just. It had fallen into ruin but was rescued during the early 1900s when the wellhead was rebuilt. Water was brought back to the well in 2002, but by artificial means so don't expect it to have the same healing powers it once had.

St Peter's Graveyard

St Peter's Cafe

Beach at Heysham

Along the lane you'll find St Peter's church, one of the oldest churches in Lancashire. It's thought to date back to the 8th century and has undergone a number of transformations during its lifetime, something that is most evident when looking at the windows, which are in a variety of different styles. As you approach the church there's a stone on your left which looks as if it has the outline of a house carved into it; this is thought to be the remains of a late 8th-century stone cross.

Within the church there are a number of coffin lids built into the walls, the most notable of which is a tall cross alongside a sword which is thought to have once been the cover for a Crusader's tomb. There are two other items to look out for while you're in there, one large and one very small. The Hogback Tombstone is a uniquely British item which shows a mix of Viking and Christian symbolism and would have originally marked an important grave. At the other end of the size scale look out for the tiny lead chalice; it was found during restoration work in the 1860 when the remains of an early priest were also uncovered.

Up on the headland behind St Peter's church are the remains of St Patrick's church and the famous stone tombs. It's likely that the two churches date back to the same period and the basic footprint of St Patrick's church is easily visible. The stone tombs are a wonderfully atmospheric point to pause, admire the bay and get a real feel for the history of the area. Although two of the graves are straight cut the other four are clearly body shaped and they each have a small socket cut at the top which would have held a wooden cross.

The end of the walk features the wonderful Near Naze lighthouse out towards the modern port. Made from local sandstone it was built in 1904 to warn small boats off the rocks near the harbour but was soon superseded by the South Pier Light and fell out of use in 1916.

St Patrick's Well

St Patrick's Church and Morecambe Bay

Satellite strolls

Heysham Moss

Tucked away behind a busy housing estate is the delightful Heysham Moss. It may not look like much at first glance but it is a hive of wild activity and is home to the very rare large heath butterfly which was successfully reintroduced to the site in 2016. It is managed by Lancashire Wildlife Trust and also boasts reed bunting, willow warblers, chiff chaffs and buzzards.

Heysham Nature Reserve

Another little gem, this time hidden away right behind the power station. This site has a small car park and a number of clearly laid out paths around the reserve, and is perfect for the bird nerd of the family. Rarities spotted here over the years include wryneck, bee-eater and night heron – so make sure you pack your binoculars!

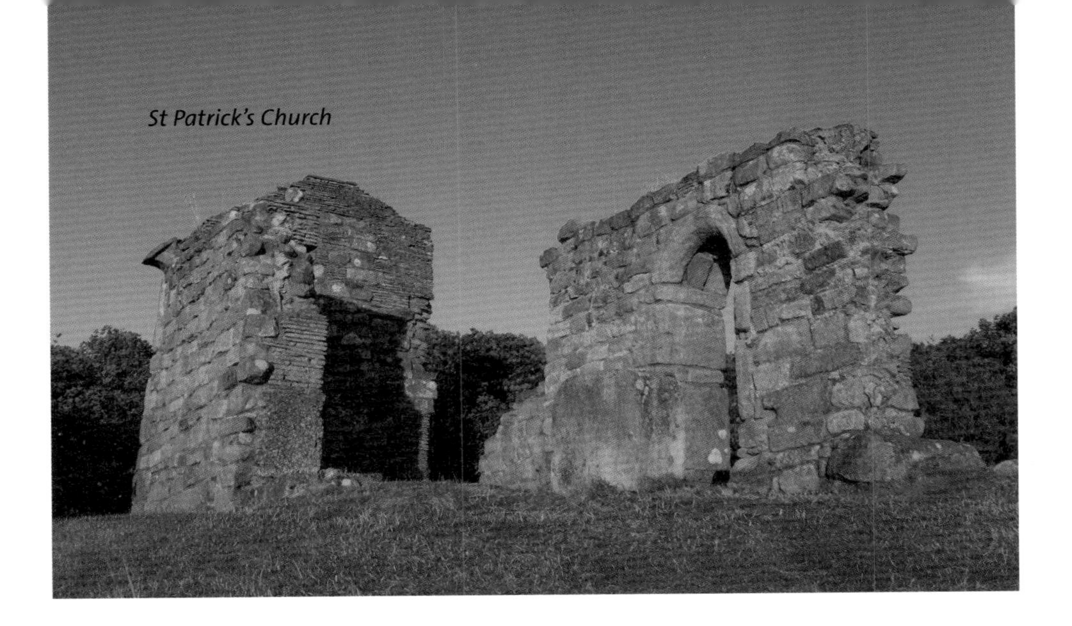
St Patrick's Church

Overton and Bazil

From Overton there's a rather lovely circular walk (easy to spot on an OS Map) around the coast at Bazil. Over recent years the tricky stiles have been replaced with kissing gates and many of these have been named to add interest to the walk – including Sol's Gate, named after an aging local retriever. When the farmer came to replace the existing stile he gave permission to convert it to a kissing gate so that Sol, and other aging and arthritic dogs, could still enjoy their walkies.

Commander Charles Gerald Forsberg memorial

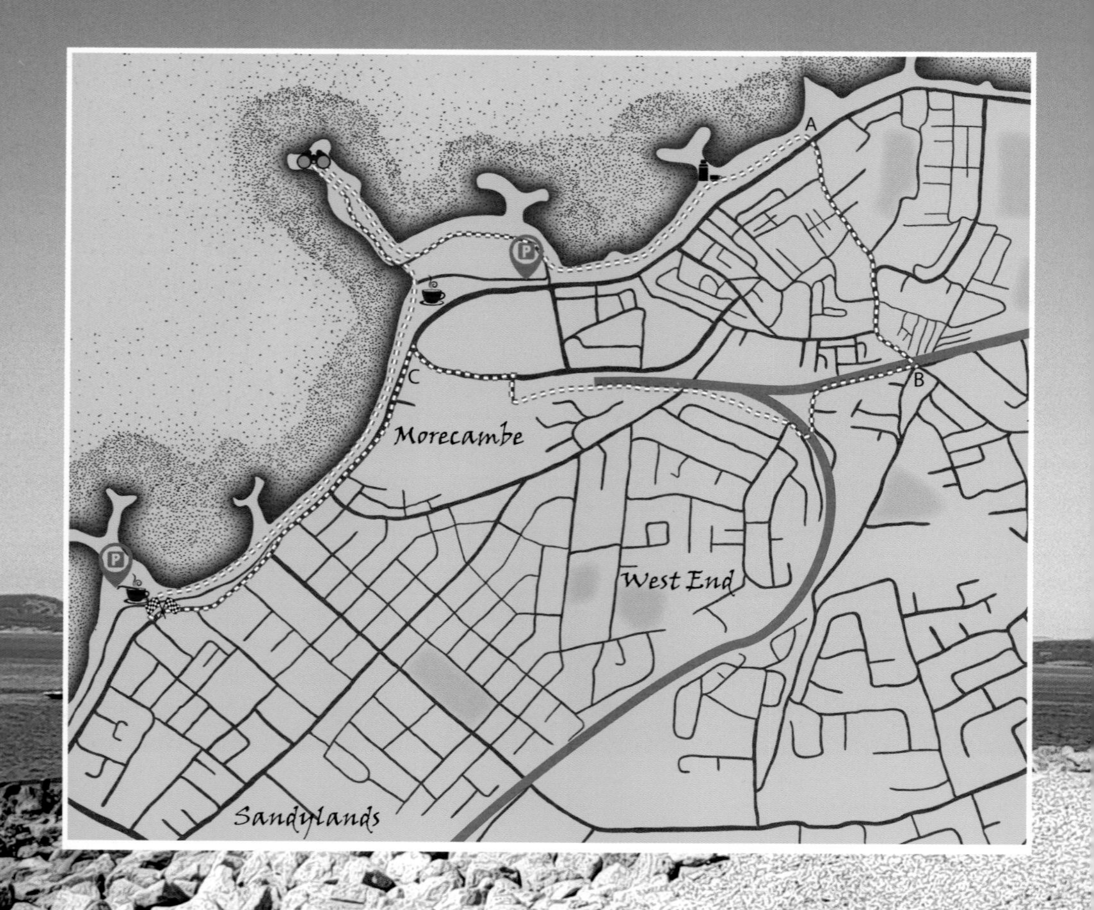

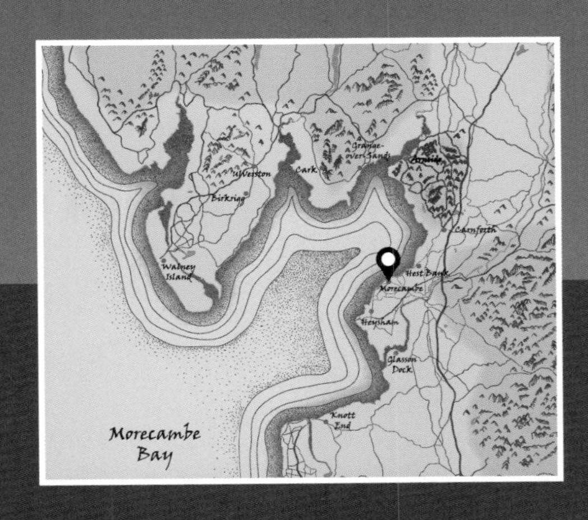

Morecambe

Route details

Start: The Battery, Morecambe

Grid Ref: SD 42139 63566

Distance: 4 miles/6.5km

Terrain: Tarmac

Difficulty: An easy to follow route along easy terrain accessible to all

Parking: Free on-road car parking near to The Battery and paid car park nearby

Public transport: Local buses

Facilities: Café at start/end of walk plus a number of cafés and excellent pubs along the route

Our top picks: The Beach Café at the start point – great views, great cakes! The Midland Hotel – a bit posh but unbeatable views, especially at sunset

Best picnic spot: Anywhere along the prom, or the lovely beach near the statue of Eric

Overview

Morecambe was once one of the UK's most popular seaside towns and it is definitely back on the up. This walk explores the social history of the town as well as some of the natural history of Morecambe Bay. This route is completely accessible to all and there are plenty of places to stop and explore along the way.

Route

From the starting point follow the prom to the Midland Hotel, turn left to explore the stone jetty then return to the prom and continue north towards the Sailing Club (**Point A**). At the roundabout just before the large white Sailing Club building turn right to leave the prom, cross the road and follow Lord Street. Remain on this road as it curves right to become Thornton Road and reaches a roundabout. Turn left here and cross the road, following the road up and over the railway bridge (**Point B**).

At the far side of the bridge turn right in front of the York Hotel to follow Schola Green Lane alongside the railway. Follow the lane as it bears left at the bottom and continue on through the white gates to cross the level crossing. Turn right and follow the cycleway towards West End Road Morecambe and remain on this until you emerge opposite Morrisons on a small retail park. Turn right and then left along the main road for a short way to reach the prom (**Point C**). Once on the prom turn left to return to your start point.

ESCAPE ROUTE: At any point return to the prom and retrace your steps to the starting point.

About the walk

What we now know as Morecambe was once three medieval settlements, Poulton, Bare and Torrisholme, and along the route of this walk we'll see evidence of these old villages, as well as more modern bits of Morecambe's history, all of which have shaped it into the town we see today.

One of the first things of interest along the prom is the rather wonderful memorial to Commander Charles Gerald Forsberg. I've known people who have lived in Morecambe for many years who are not aware of this memorial, which is a shame because it's so lovely. Born in Canada, Commander Forsberg broke the England–France cross-channel record in 1957, and the next year he became the first person to make a two-way crossing of Morecambe Bay. In total he crossed the bay 29 times and, following his death in 2000, this memorial was given to the town by the British Long Distance Swimming Association.

The most striking building along the prom has to be the Midland Hotel, and it's an easy landmark to pick out from right across the bay. It was built in 1933 by the London, Midland and Scottish Railway on a site previously occupied by another hotel originally called the North Western Hotel, but later renamed the Midland Hotel. Following its renovation (it re-opened in 2008) the views on the inside are as spectacular as those on the outside and it's the perfect place to sit and enjoy a cup of tea and a slice of cake, or something a little stronger,

Midland Hotel

The Station, Morecambe

as you watch the sun set over the bay. Like many large hotels and houses it was requisitioned during World War II and became a military hospital, and much later on, during the 1980s, it was used as a set for the TV series of Agatha Christie's Poirot.

Further on along the prom is a statue to the wonderfully funny Eric Morecambe. Eric was born in the town in May 1926, famously taking the town's name as his stage name, and the town have loved him for it ever since. The statue, designed by Graham Ibbeson, was unveiled by Her Majesty the Queen in July 1999. It is surrounded by a pavement full of his catchphrases ("He's not going to sell much ice-cream going at that speed, is he!") and is very difficult to get a decent photo of as it's constantly surrounded by people posing next to him. In October 2014 everyone was horrified when someone sawed through his leg and attempted to steal 'our Eric' – we assume they dropped him when they realised just how heavy he was. He was sent away to London to be restored and was welcomed back into his rightful place on 11th December 2014; it was a bitterly cold day but a good crowd turned out to see him, and his widow, Joan, took the time to speak to everyone there, despite the freezing conditions.

As you leave the prom and walk along Lord Street you're entering one of the oldest parts of the town, with the lovely row of old fisherman's cottages giving a glimpse of the town's past when fishing was the

Winter Gardens, Morecambe

principal local occupation. The Shrimp Shop on the corner still offers a selection of sea foods and pots of Morecambe Bay's famous potted brown shrimps. A very short detour along Poulton Street will take you to a small park area with an old stone archway in the centre; this is all that remains of Poulton Hall, once the finest building in the village, but sadly demolished in 1932.

In the early nineteenth century Poulton was less popular than Sunderland just to the south when it came to bathing holidays, but by the mid 1800s communication and transportation routes had improved, leading to the town's growth, and by the late 1800s and early 1900s it was the resort of choice for thousands of working class families across the north.

The old Odeon Cinema at the corner of Thornton Road and Lancaster Road is clearly in need of some TLC, but underneath its battle-scarred exterior is a wonderful old building. Odeon Cinemas understood the importance of corporate branding and had a very specific and easily recognisable cinema design. This one opened in 1937 and closed in February 1976 and since then has been used as a DIY store – you'd think with all those DIY products so close to hand someone could put them to good use to brighten up such a lovely old building!

Another wonderful structure on the way back to the start/end point of the route is the magnificent Winter Gardens, which is incredibly special and rare and retains many of its original Victorian features, including a superb mosaic floor and spectacular marble steps leading up to the auditorium. It opened in 1897 and in its heyday played host to anyone who was anyone, including Laurel and Hardy, Edward Elgar and, of course, Morecambe and Wise. Although it closed for a period of time in the late 1970s, in 1986 a group of volunteers got together

Old swimming pool, Morecambe (and possible Eden Project North)

to protect and restore the venue and their hard work is paying off; these days it is still open and houses a range of activities and shows throughout the year.

Of course you may not want to visit there alone as it is renowned for being one of the most haunted theatres in Lancashire, with numerous stories of people being poked, prodded, slapped and pushed. One ghost is said to be that of a seamstress who never achieved her dream of becoming a dancer and so still haunts the dressing rooms, but you're not safe anywhere; people have reported ghostly goings on in the auditorium, the stairwells and the bar. Thankfully the many events they still hold there are very popular so you're sure to have someone to hang on to, just in case...

Midland Hotel

Eric Morecambe

Satellite strolls

Happy Mount Park

At the far end of the prom is Happy Mount Park and pretty much everyone who grew up in or around Morecambe has happy childhood memories of visits there. Today it is still hugely popular and is packed through the sunny summer holidays with plenty of activities for all ages, as well as some gardens and quiet corners for those who are in search of a little peace.

The Greenway

I'm not going to pretend that this is the prettiest walk in Morecambe, but it is a fascinating link between Morecambe and Lancaster. It's very popular with cyclists and during the autumn months there are plenty of blackberry bushes to plunder along the way. The Greenway is clearly marked on OS Maps and runs from adjacent to Morecambe railway station, past White Lund trading estate and into Lancaster over Millennium Bridge.

Williamson Park

Just a short drive away in Lancaster, Williamson Park offers some of the finest views out across the whole of Morecambe Bay. The stunning grounds are open throughout the year and there's a bustling café, a butterfly house and the striking Ashton Memorial to explore. If you're visiting during the summer months check out The Dukes website (www.dukes-lancaster.org) for details of outdoor theatre in the park – the most glorious way to pass a warm summer's evening.

The Old Mill
A
B
Red Bank Farm
Bolton
Bolton Town End
Morecambe Lodge
Inglebrick
C
Hest Bank

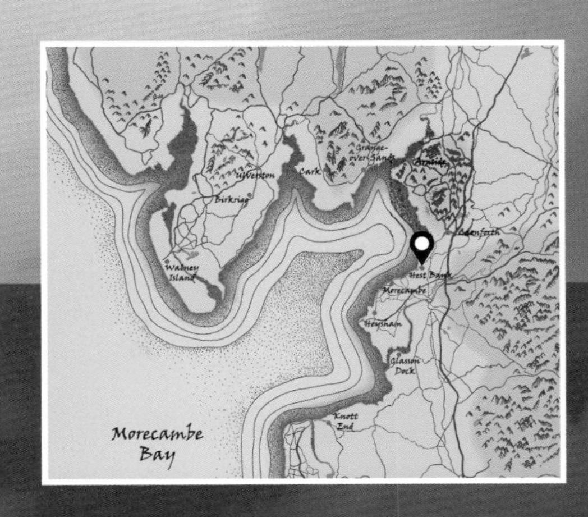

Hest Bank

Route details

Start: Sea Shore car park, Hest Bank

Grid Ref: SD 46836 66595

Distance: 4 miles /6.5km

Terrain: Tarmac, hard track

Difficulty: A mainly flat route, can be exposed along the shore section in blustery weather

Parking: Ample free parking along the shore

Public transport: Various local buses

Facilities: Café at the start and garden centre with facilities en route

Our top picks: The Shore Café Hest Bank – a firm favourite of ours for a brew with a view. The Royal, Hest Bank – a dog friendly pub, right on the canal, with a fine beer garden

Best picnic spot: On the benches along the coast at the start/end of the walk

Overview

This is definitely a walk of two halves. The first half is a gentle stroll along the seafront with far-reaching views down to Morecambe and up to the Lake District fells in the north. The second half is an idyllic walk along a canal towpath packed full of interesting flora, fauna and history.

Route

From the car park walk north along the shoreline with the sea on your left. At the next small car park take the signed route leading right over a small stile into a field and continue following the shoreline along the field as the path gently rises. At the far end drop down, crossing another stile, and follow the white gravel path leading through the caravan park and back to the shore (**Point A**). Bear right here to follow the embankment running parallel to the road and remain on this embankment as it leaves the road, crosses a small area of boardwalk then rejoins another road just in front of a large white house.

Turn right here and follow the road past the garden centre and through a small estate to reach the main road (**Point B**). Turn right along the road for around 10m then cross carefully (it can be a busy area) to take the small gravel track leading up between two houses. At the top of the track turn right to drop down to the canal towpath. Remain on the towpath until you reach bridge 118. Just beyond the bridge take the steps leading down to the road and follow Station Road away from the canal and back to the level crossing at Hest Bank (**Point C**). Return to the shoreline and your starting point.

ESCAPE ROUTE: At the first campsite turn right to follow the lane through the site and up to the main road, then turn right along the road to return to your start point (1.8 miles).

About the walk

If you're visiting at low tide, pause for a moment and look out across the sands slightly to the north. You should be able to spot the remains of an old stone structure jutting out into the bay; if you have time it's worth taking a closer look as it's easily accessible at low tides (though please do check tide times and keep and eye out for water creeping in around behind you). This is Hest Bank Jetty and although it dates back to 1820 it became submerged beneath the sands and only reappeared following a storm in 2002. The jetty was built "...to enable small coasting vessels from Liverpool and Glasgow to discharge their cargoes at Hest Bank, from which place they could be transported north and south by the canal. This traffic ceased after the opening of the railway in 1846. The remains of the jetty are now some distance from the shore owing to encroachments by the sea." (*The Victoria County History*, Farrer & Brownhill, 1914). It was most likely built by the Hest Bank Canal Company to support increased sea trade, although in 1831 the warehouse was sold and by 1845 it had become a working farm, so it doesn't appear as if the increase in trade was as big as had been hoped for.

The area around the jetty is littered with fragments of pottery, china and glass, which still appear all these years later thanks to the ever-shifting sands. The recovery of bullets, some of them quite rare and unusual, suggests it was also used as target practice at some point, possibly for a military group in the late 1800s.

Finds from the pier aren't the only interesting things found on the beaches around Morecambe Bay; in 2016 a couple walking along the beach a little further south discovered a very smelly and slightly sticky 'stone' which turned out to be an incredibly rare piece of ambergris, otherwise known as whale vomit. Although it sounds revolting it's actually used in the perfume industry (where it adds a 'unique musky aroma' to very expensive perfumes – I'll take their word for it) and is worth an absolute fortune – in the past pieces have sold for up to £120,000 so it's worth keeping your eyes open.

Just before you reach the stile leading down into Red Bank Farm campsite (home the wonderful Archers cafe if you fancy an early brew stop) follow the fence line left towards the edge of the small cliff. Here you'll find the Praying Shell sculpture which was created by local artist Anthony Padgett and unveiled in November 2013. Although it marks a spot near to where 23 Chinese cockle-pickers lost their lives in 2004 Anthony had the idea for the piece many years earlier and describes it as being a symbol of reflection, renewal and environmental integration.

The canal stretch of this walk offers wonderful views out across the bay, which is why we included another section in the Carnforth walk (see p.53). Canal towpaths are excellent routes as they're usually well maintained, nice and flat, and can generally be relied upon to have a decent pub or two along the way, thanks to our thirsty canal-trading ancestors.

The Lancaster Canal was originally built as a rescue measure to "save Lancaster". Historically, goods had come in and out of the city via the River Lune, but as both ships and cargoes got bigger navigating the Lune became problematic, so the merchants of the time proposed a canal which would ultimately run from Kendal all the way down through Lancaster, Preston and Leyland to join the Leeds and Liverpool Canal.

Lancaster Canal

Plans were drawn up but the dock at Glasson (see Glasson Dock Walk) proved more popular so the canal idea was dropped. Or mostly dropped: one group were still very keen on the canal and continued pushing forward with their plans, but this time with a slightly different route. Instead of focusing on bringing goods in from the sea, they focused on transporting coal and limestone from the local quarries. Construction began in 1792 and hit financial problems pretty much from the start; by 1819 it was eventually opened through to Kendal, followed in 1826 by the link to Glasson Dock, but the whole canal was never completed and a five-mile section south of Preston was only ever connected using a tramway.

Although a large chunk of the canal remained unconnected to the main canal network, it flourished for a while until the railways ultimately took over, although not without a fight. The canal owners cut prices to lure passengers and cargo onto the canals and keep them away from the railways, but in 1885 they eventually lost out and the Lancaster Canal Company finally closed.

Since then the canal has been carved up and broken down, leaving the sporadic pattern of water we now see today, particularly in the northern stretches. The good news is that in 2002 the Ribble Link Trust won sufficient funding from the Millennium Commission to finally link the lower stretches of the Lancaster Canal to the national waterway network. If you enjoy spending time around the canals then look out for Kingfisher Cruises in Lancaster, who run a variety of canal boat tours, including horse-drawn excursions.

The railway crossing near to the start/end point of the walk is part of the vital West Coast Mainline, with trains thundering past throughout the day and night. In May 1965 it was the site of a notable accident when the rear four coaches of the sleeper from Glasgow to London derailed due to a broken piece of track. Despite the fact that the train was going at full speed, of the 114 people on board at the time only 11 suffered any sort of injury, just 2 of whom were detained in hospital and both of them were home again within 3 days. If you look up old news footage online and see the state of the carriages, this was nothing short of miraculous.

Satellite strolls

Nether Kellet

This is an unusual satellite stroll as, I'll be honest, it's not the prettiest of villages, but it is very interesting: Nether Kellet is a 'doubly thankful' village. After World War I, fifty three 'Thankful Villages' were identified in England where all of those serving returned home safely. After World War II, sixteen villages were identified as 'doubly thankful', signifying that all those serving in that war too came home safely. What's interesting is to walk around a village which has no war memorial; we don't realise what a part of our fabric they are until we visit somewhere where there is no need for one.

Hest Bank Jetty

Lancaster Canal

Although two of our walks cover different stretches of the canal, there is still a lot more to discover. On the stretch through Lancaster there are a number of information boards highlighting different aspects of the history and identifying interesting buildings along the route.

Lune Valley

Perfect for longer walks, or again the section through Lancaster is wonderful to explore. Particularly worth a visit is the Lune Aqueduct, which was designed by John Rennie with its stunning five-arch span, and is Grade I listed. It is said that one of the reasons that the Lancaster Canal was never completed was because the spend on this bridge spiralled out of control; it eventually cost around £50,000 to complete, which is the equivalent of just over £3 million pounds today.

Egret

Morecambe Bay and Cumbrian Fells

Hest Bank Jetty

THE
CANAL TURN
PUB & DINING

Galley Hall
Hagg Wood
Hagg Farm
Carnforth
Hunting Hill
R. Keer
Edenbrook Farm
Marsh House Farm
A
C
Crag Bank
Bay View Holiday Park
Detron Gate Farm
Barker Bridge
Thwaite House Farm
Mount Pleasant
B

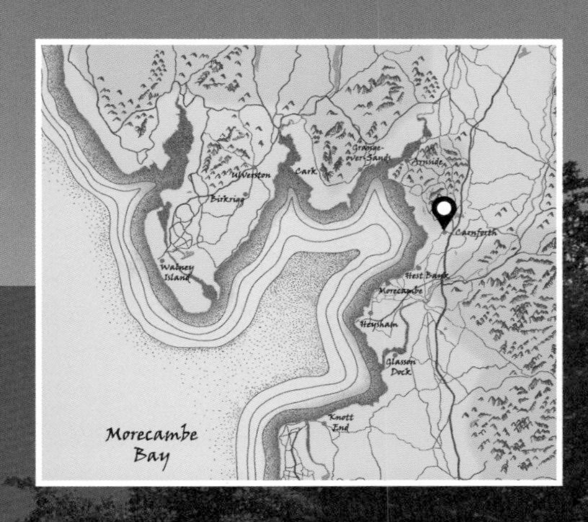

Carnforth

Route details

Start: Carnforth Railway Station

Grid Ref: SD 49737 70676

Distance: 5 miles/8km

Terrain: Tarmac, hard track, field

Difficulty: A flat and straightforward walk with one small section across farmland

Parking: Pay and display car park at station

Public transport: Trains and regular local buses

Facilities: Plenty of local facilities in Carnforth and some along the route

Our top picks: The Royal Station Hotel Carnforth – handy for the station if your train is delayed. The Canal Turn – great place to stop for lunch and watch the boats drift by

Best picnic spot: Nice spot next to the canal near the start of the walk

Overview

Carnforth and the surrounding area is a place where history and geology collide. This walk explores a good mix of modern history in the station and canal, as well as the more ancient history along the shoreline.

Route

From the station walk up along Market Street towards the traffic lights, passing the Carnforth Bookshop on your left. Cross over the lights and continue up to the bridge then drop down right to join the canal, signed 'Canal Towpath Lancaster' (**Point A).**

Immediately after bridge 127 take the small stone stile on the right and cross up and over the bridge, then turn right to follow the hard track and keep right to follow a smaller footpath leading alongside the other bank of the canal. Keep to this path as it bears left and leads up away from the canal, through a metal kissing gate, along an enclosed path and out onto a tarmac lane; follow the lane down past Thwaite Brow Woods.

After crossing the canal bridge keep left, passing through a gate back to the towpath and turn left to pass under the bridge you just walked over (**Point B**). Just after bridge 126 turn left to follow the path dropping down to the car park. Cross the road (care!) and turn left to follow the road to the campsite entrance. Turn right into the campsite then, just past the outbuilding, turn right to cross a stile and follow an enclosed footpath. At the end of the path cross another stile and continue around to the right before bearing diagonally left down across the field to reach the stile and metal gate in the far left-hand corner.

Continue on, keeping to the left-hand field boundary of the next two fields until you cross a stile onto an old tarmac lane, then bear right here to follow the lane to the road (**Point C**). At the road go straight ahead, following the road as it climbs slightly, and then remain on this road all the way around the headland and back towards Carnforth. When you reach the main road next to the railway, turn right to return to the station.

ESCAPE ROUTE: At any available point along the canal towpath section return to the main road and follow it back into Carnforth.

About the walk

I can't write about a walk that starts at Carnforth station without mentioning *Brief Encounter*, a wonderful old film starring Trevor Howard and Celia Johnson. In the film Laura (Celia Johnson) has her safe, but predictable, life turned upside down by a chance encounter with Alec (Trevor Howard). Released in 1945 it's all very much of the era with lots of long, pained, embraces and wonderfully clipped English accents. Many of the exterior station shots were filmed at Carnforth and if you wander over to the platforms you'll spot the ramps they hurried along and the large, distinguished, station clock, still keeping time today. The film is based on a Noel Coward short story called *Still Life*, which was a little bit racier than the film.

Lancaster Canal

Canal Turn, Carnforth

There's a permanent *Brief Encounter* exhibition at the Heritage Centre and they have lovingly recreated the tea rooms from the film (originally these scenes were shot on a specially created set at Denham studios,) complete with the iconic hot water urn and till. It's the perfect place for tea and cake before and/or after the walk – just beware of getting grit in your eye from a passing train.

Away from the town the route follows the Lancaster Canal, with more far-reaching views across Morecambe Bay (for more about the history of the canal see Hest Bank Walk). Just after you cross the canal and walk along the far bank you'll come across a number of coke ovens (undergoing restoration at the time of writing). These are being rescued by a local group called the Friends of Carnforth Coke Ovens and during 2016 they embarked on clearing away the vegetation, then later that year an archaeological study was carried out on the site.

The ovens were built soon after the northern section of the canal opened in 1819 and would have been used to convert coal, brought to the area along the canal, into coke for use locally. The ovens are constructed in the Beehive Kiln style, and have been in use across Europe since the middle ages, with the coke-making process taking two to three days to complete.

Just beyond the coke ovens, as the path begins to rise, there's an interesting field boundary on the left. I've not been able to pinpoint how old this particular boundary is but stone or rock boundaries of this type are examples of the earliest forms of field boundary. These would often be known as 'clearance walls' as they were made from the stones and rocks dug out from the field and cleared to the sides. To begin with they would simply have been used to contain livestock, but as land ownership took shape boundaries were used to mark out the extremities of land belonging to the landowner. Historically 'common land' was controlled by the lord of the manor, but as a more nomadic life gave way to permanent settlements, agricultural use and improved farming methods, so land needed to be better defined and delineated. Although some enclosure acts date back as far as the twelfth century it was during the eighteenth and nineteenth centuries that they started coming thick and fast, sometimes resulting in the ambitious and gravity defying walls we still see clinging to the sides of fells in the Lake District today.

If you have the time it's worth taking a small detour into Thwaite Brow Woods as you drop back down towards the canal, once an area of common land but now a 14-acre community woodland looked after by a group of local volunteers. Amongst the 'regular suspects' of holly and brambles you can also find rare gems such as white violets and sand leeks, and it's definitely worth a few extra yards on the walk (although it is a little hilly!).

Although the latter stages of the walk are along a tarmac lane it's generally very quiet and, for me, rather atmospheric. In his best-selling Gothic novel *The Loney*, Andrew Michael Hurley describes the carved away silts around Morecambe Bay as being "...haunted by time. Time didn't leak away as it should. There was nowhere for it to go..." which really describes the years of history sealed in the deep-sided, silty banks of the River Keer as it reaches the bay along this stretch. It is the River Keer which most likely gave Carnforth its name; the town was a crossing point, or ford, and it's thought that Keer-ford became Carnforth over the years, although an alternate possibility is that it derives from the Celtic words Cairn (pile of stones or rocks) and Forth (safe harbour).

The silts are a haven for an array of invertebrates which, in turn, attract a wide range of water birds. If you're visiting during the spring or autumn, time your walk for dawn or dusk and you'll be treated to hundreds, and occasionally thousands, of birds migrating around the bay.

As you return towards the town you'll notice that there are quite a number of railway bridges, which reflect Carnforth's importance as a busy railway junction in the mid-1800s.The Carnforth Haematite Iron Company was based in the town, as was a steelworks, and the town grew rapidly from a population of just 300 in 1850 to over 3000 by 1900. Sadly, during the twentieth century things went into decline, with the ironworks closing in 1929, and eventually the railway engine sheds, the town's other major employer, following suit in the latter half of the century. Today the West Coast Mainline thunders through the station; it doesn't stop there but it is still an important connecting point for trains to Barrow, Lancaster and Leeds. And it still has an excellent tea room.

Satellite strolls

Thwaite Brow Woods

As I mentioned above, Thwaite Brow Woods make for a lovely diversion or a short stroll in their own right, and there is limited road parking in the nearby housing estate. There are a few short walks signposted through the woods, but it can be boggy underfoot after heavy rain.

Warton Crag

There's a lovely big car park at the foot of Warton Crag and an easy to follow, if somewhat strenuous, walk up and around the crags. On a clear day the views are spectacular and there's a good variety of wildlife to look out for too.

Leighton Moss

Home to some of the finest cake, and of course birdwatching opportunities, in the region, a visit to Leighton Moss is always worth it. It's free to enter if you're just visiting the café but there is a small charge to wander around the main site and visit the hides. Well worth a visit in the autumn when the Moss is famed for its starling murmurations.

Kent Viaduct, Arnside

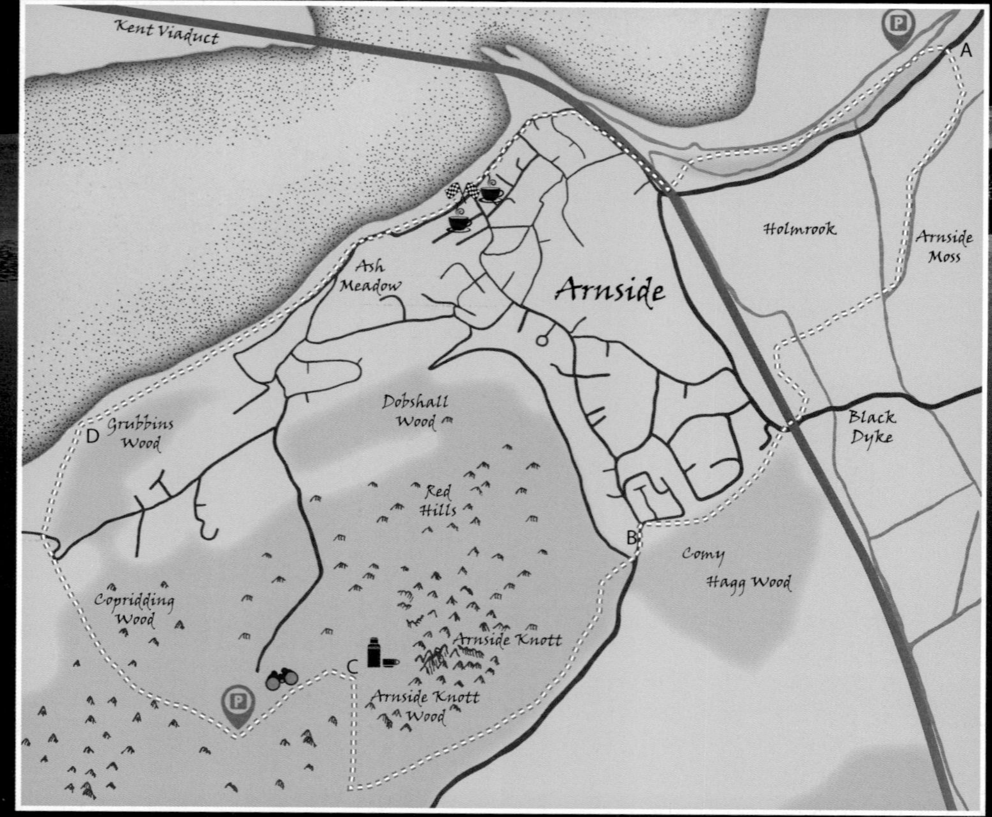

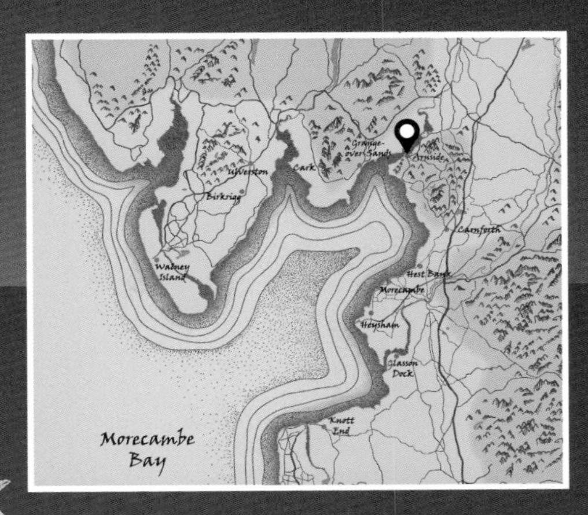

Arnside Bank

Route details

Start: Albion Pub Arnside

Grid Ref: SD 45603 78765

Distance: 5 miles/8km

Terrain: Tarmac, hard track, field, beach

Difficulty & Duration: A longer walk with a couple of long steady uphill sections

Parking: Ample free parking along the shore

Public transport: Arnside station and various local buses

Facilities: A range of cafés and pubs in the village

Our top picks: The Albion – you just can't beat it for great food, beer and views. The Old Bakehouse – prefect for procuring local pork pies for your picnic

Best picnic spot: The view point on Arnside Knott

Overview

This walk covers an impressive variety of terrains within a relatively short distance. There's ample wildlife to look out for, intriguing corners of the village to explore and superb view across to the Lake District fells from the view point at the top of Arnside Knott.

Route

From the Albion Pub follow the road around to the station (keeping the estuary on your left). Enter the station, cross over the footbridge then leave the station, turning right to follow the embankment alongside the estuary. Remain on this embankment until you reach the small parking area on your right; turn right here, cross the small car park and the road to reach the farm gate on the far side (**Point A**).

Pass through the gate and follow the path as it bears right and then left and right again, winding through the fields towards Arnside Knott. At the end of the path cross the stile and turn right to reach the enclosed path towards Back Dyke Road. At the end of the path turn left immediately *before* the railway crossing to follow the path alongside the railway, emerging in a layby. Turn right here; cross the level crossing then take the signed footpath leading left, along a short track and over a stone stile up towards Silverdale Road. Remain on this path as it climbs through the woods and continue on as it emerges onto a tarmac lane, following the signed route on up to the top road (**Point B**).

Cross the road and turn left to reach the gated entrance to Red Hills Woods. Enter the woods then turn left to follow the woodland path running parallel to the road. Keep straight on through a small wooden gate and continue on the path, remaining on it as it climbs gradually uphill. After half a mile, when you reach a distinctive white gravel crossing track, turn right and follow the track sharply uphill. At the crest of the hill turn left to follow another broad track into woodland, then bear right to continue through the woods and out through the gate to the viewpoint on your left (**Point C**).

Continue on past the viewpoint, keeping to the small track on the left as it drops down to a small wooden gate. Pass through the gate and continue on, passing two benches on your left, and remain on the track as it descends to a wall. Turn right along the broad track to reach a large wooden gate, pass through the gate and turn left following the signed route to Copridding Wood, remaining on this path as it curves right, crossing other paths and dropping down towards the seashore. Continue on through a small wooden gate to follow an enclosed path

to a tarmac lane. Turn left to follow the lane downhill. When you reach the shoreline (**Point D**) turn right to follow the estuary back into Arnside.

ESCAPE ROUTE: After crossing the railway keep to the road as it bears right and remain on it back into Arnside (2.8 miles).

About the walk

Arnside is such a visited spot and is so often written about that it's hard to find something to tell you that you don't know already about this beautiful seaside village, but I'll give it a go! As with many towns and villages along this stretch of coastline, there wasn't much of Arnside until about 1845. It was a sleepy collection of fishing huts, water would have come from nearby springs and wells – many of them still marked on today's maps – and trade was carried out locally, with routes being established between the local villages.

The first spurt of growth for Arnside came from boat building or, more specifically, the building of shallow fishing boats known as 'nobbies' which were ideal for navigating the shallow waters around Morecambe

Bay. It is even said that Arthur Ransome's boat 'Swallow' was built here (he sailed it in the Lake District and it is the boat he described in *Swallows and Amazons*). The village's growth can be seen in what is now a parade of shops opposite the pier; look up above the shop fronts and you'll spot some wonderful architecture. The pub just along the prom towards the chip shop – Ye Olde Fighting Cocks – was originally built in 1660 and still has the old cock fighting pit under its floor.

In 1857 the railway arrived, and in 1870 the road to Sandside was completed, opening Arnside up to both trade and visitors, and it was as popular with the Victorians as it is today. Sadly, the Hincaster branch of the line, which ran from Arnside into Kendal, closed in 1942, but it left behind the embankment along the estuary which makes up the first part of this walk.

The 'off road' section of the route passes through an interesting area of flat land adjacent to Silverdale Moss; the route gives both an interesting view of the village and, during the autumn, a chance to spot starling murmurations. Starlings, like all wildlife, are never 100% predictable and although they usually settle at nearby Leighton Moss, some years they prefer Silverdale Moss. I remember one evening a couple of years ago when me & Steve took a chance detour to the Moss and were rewarded with our very own murmuration with not another soul around. Magical!

Arnside Knott is rightly famed for its magnificent views across the estuary and up to the Lakeland fells beyond. In hillwalking circles it is also renowned for being the lowest of the 'Marilyns' – defined as being a hill or mountain in the British Isles with a prominence of at least 150m (regardless of the overall height of the hill/mountain). 'Marilyns' came into being in 1992 when Alan Dawson published *The Relative Hills of Britain* and listed all the qualifying 'peaks' – he named them 'Marilyns' as a funny counterpoint to the 'Munros' of Scotland ('Munros' are defined as being mountains above 3000ft and were named after Sir Hugh Munro who first proposed this list).

Both Arnside Knott and the surrounding woodlands are home to some of the best butterfly sites in the north of England. There is still a profusion of wildflowers to be seen in the fields and hedgerows, especially in places like Grubbins Wood, and these attract a wonderful array of butterflies on warm, sunny days. A couple of the rarest to look out for are the high brown fritillary and the Scotch argus.

Viewpoint, Arnside Knott

The Scotch argus, as the name suggests, is mostly found north of the border, but Arnside Knott is one of just two sites in England where it can be found. The high brown fritillary's two favourite habitats are bracken and limestone, both of which Arnside Knott has in abundance. Sadly, today there are only 50 sites in the UK where it can be found and conservationists are battling hard to save it from extinction.

As you walk back along the estuary towards the village, pause for a moment to look out across the bay; this was once the equivalent of the M6 into what is now Cumbria. It was far from safe and predictable but was a quicker and easier option than hacking around the boggy, dense woodlands surrounding the bay. Today it is dangerous to set foot on the sands without an appropriate guide, and there are many official Cross Bay Walks throughout the summer months raising a lot of money for great causes.

Arnside Pier

National Trust
Arnside Knott

Albion Pub, Arnside

Historically, monks would often have been the guides across the sands, with posts left out to mark the best routes. The problem is that the sands of the bay are continually shifting so what would have been a good route one day may have changed by the next morning. When the tides began to return, making a crossing dangerous, the monks blew a horn to warn people, while today a siren is sounded from Arnside around 2 hours before high tide to warn anyone foolish enough to be out on the sands alone.

Satellite strolls

Silverdale Moss

Silverdale Moss is almost eerily atmospheric, especially at dusk. There's parking along the road near Gait Barrows, or several public footpaths across the fields from Arnside and Silverdale. It's just a short walk but is peaceful and rarely explored by others so you're likely to have the place to yourself.

Dallam Park

There are several lovely, gentle walks through Dallam Park and it's the perfect place to spot fallow deer, though it's best not to have your dog with you as they are easily spooked. There are a couple of large herds of deer and if you're lucky you can spot the stags, often down near the river.

Silverdale Cove

You can't beat a nice walk along the beach and Silverdale Cove is perfect for exploring, especially if you have children with you. There are rock pools and thousands of different stones and pebbles to rummage through, as well as some interesting small caves to venture into. Just be sure to keep an eye on the tides.

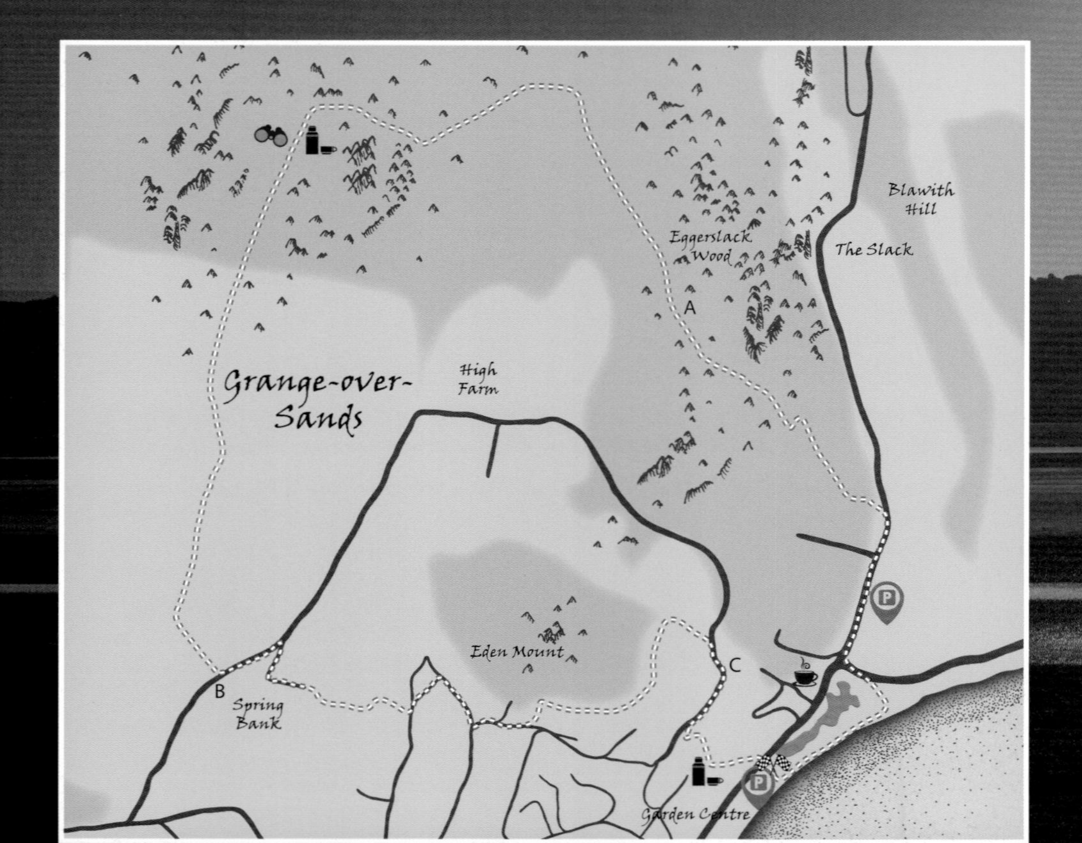
Blawith
Hill
Eggerslack
Wood
The Slack
A
Grange-over-
Sands
High
Farm
Eden Mount
C
B
Spring
Bank
Garden Centre

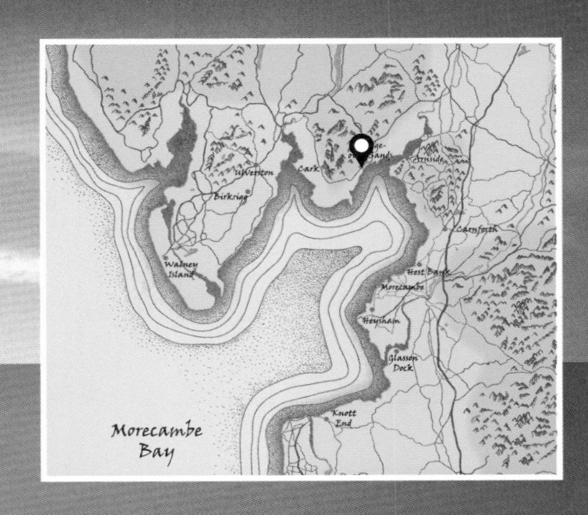

Grange-over-Sands

Route details

Start: Promenade car park

Grid Ref: SD 40896 77935

Distance: 4 miles/6.5km

Terrain: Tarmac, hard track

Difficulty: A more challenging route in terms of both the terrain and navigation

Parking: Pay and display car park on Grange prom

Public transport: Trains and regular local buses

Facilities: Plenty of facilities within Grange plus a few along the route

Our top picks: The Hazelmere Café – takeaway or eat in, it's all divine! Higginson's butchers – home of the Huntsman Pie; once tasted, never forgotten

Best picnic spot: Top of Hampsfell – you can shelter in the Hospice if it's windy, or the secret picnic spot towards the end of the walk, complete

Overview

Although this is a bit more involved route navigationally, the ancient woodlands it passes through are exceptional and there are spectacular views from the Hospice (a folly on top of Hampsfell). There are seats at the Hospice where you can enjoy a packed lunch either inside or out, and a secret picnic spot on the way back down with far-reaching views across Morecambe Bay.

Route

From the car park pass under the railway bridge and onto the prom. Turn left and follow the prom to the station then left to pass underneath the railway to the car park. Cross the car park to the road and turn left to reach a small traffic island, then turn right here and walk up Windermere Road. After the last house on the left look for the small gap in the wall on the left signposted to Hampsfell, pass through this and follow the path, rising uphill through the woods. Continue following the waymarked route – keeping straight on as you reach the old settling pools (**Point A**) – and remain on this route all the way to the wall and step stile at the end of the woodland.

Cross the stile and follow the path leading directly away from the wall uphill, bear slight left as you near the crags and continue straight on, uphill, until you reach a large stone step stile over a wall. Cross the stile and turn right to follow the wall upwards, remaining on the path as it leads over limestone pavement to the Hospice.

As you face the entrance to the Hospice follow the path leading away to the left and continue on, over another big stone step stile, to a large fork. Bear left here to follow the track leading away and around the left-hand side of the hillside ahead. Continue on this path, over another stile and out across the field, until it drops to a small cutting. Turn left here to reach a gate onto a small tarmac lane (**Point B**), then left along the lane following it down then around to the right, and remain on it as it turns left and drops to the farm. Continue following the signed route through the farm, over a small hill and along a small passageway to a narrow lane.

Turn left along the lane and then right at the end, dropping downhill to another road. Turn left here and follow the road down, continuing straight on when the road turns sharp right next to Charney Well. After a few yards follow the waymarked path on the left leading into the woods. Continue on upwards until you reach another path then turn right and follow the path beneath the limestone crags. Remain on this path below and then up through the crags and continue on the waymarked route, keeping right at 2 forks, until you reach a wooden gate.

Pass through the gate and continue on to the road, then follow the road down to a T-junction (**Point C**). Turn right here and follow the road until you reach a signed route leading left along a tarmac path (Main Street). After about 20m turn right, dropping down a gravel track and follow it down towards the road, ignoring any sharp right or left turns (look for the 1st turning right, it leads up to the secret picnic spot – a small car park and with picnic benches and very pretty views). When

Eggerslack Woods

Holme Island, the Marine Residence of A. Brogden, Esq., M.P.

Hampsfell Hospice

you reach the road, cross over, turn right, then immediately left down into the car park and return to the start of the walk.

ESCAPE ROUTE: At the settling pools (**Point A**) turn hard left to follow the path up through the woods, and continue until you reach a tarmac lane. Turn left here to follow the lane downhill, passing the Hampsfield House Hotel, until you reach **(Point C)** then follow the remainder of the route back to the car park (1.8 miles).

About the walk

There used to be sand at Grange, honest there did, but the River Kent regularly shifts its track and, over recent years, has moved more towards the Arnside side of the bay. This has resulted in the salt marsh around the shores at Grange extending to the point where some witty folks call it Grange-over-Grass.

Over the past 150 years or so the shoreline has changed dramatically, and not only as a response to the sands. If you take a look at old maps of the area you'll see that Holme Island looks a lot further away from the shore than it is today, and that's because the arrival of the railways in 1897 radically altered things. Prior to then the tides came in a lot further – in fact there's a small group of houses on a sharp bend on Windermere Road known as The Slack, as this is where the highest tides reached. The houses along the bottom of Windermere Road still have Morecambe Bay silts and sands just below the soil in their

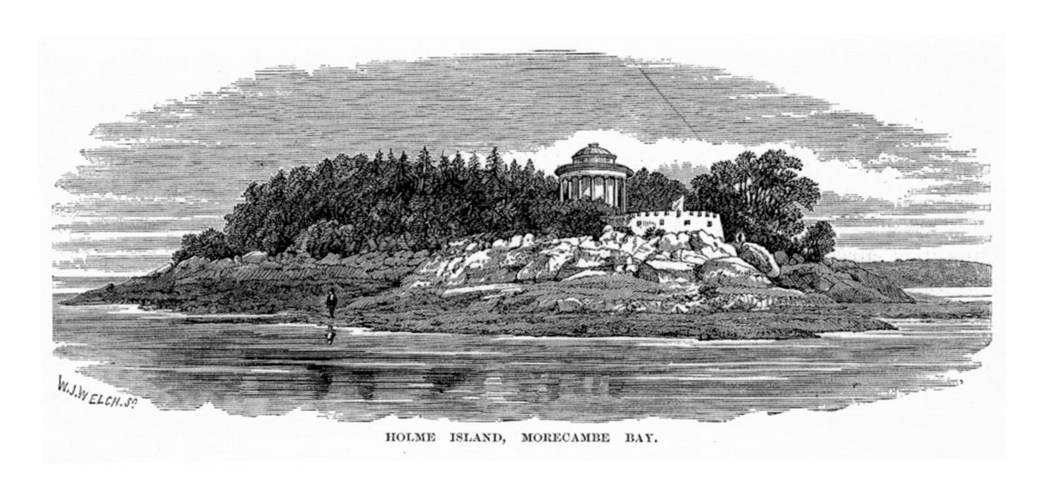

HOLME ISLAND, MORECAMBE BAY.

garden. When the embankment and prom was built for the railway it immediately stopped the tide coming any further along the valley.

Holme Island itself has a lot of interesting history associated with it; it's in private hands now so we can't visit it, but there are excellent views of it from the promenade. Local legend says that it was given as a gift to the man who shot the last wolf in England (on nearby Humphrey Head) – they clearly had a different view on conservation back then! For many years it was owned by the Brogden family who were involved in the building of the railway, and who also built the causeway, allowing permanent access to the island. There's a fake Roman temple on the island known as the Temple of Vesta, and also a smugglers cave used hundreds of years ago for stashing whisky and brandy being smuggled in from Ireland.

The Hospice on the top of Hampsfell is Grade II listed and was built in 1846 by the Reverend Thomas Remington, vicar of Cartmel, to offer shelter to fell walkers. It offers some of the finest views in Cumbria and on a clear day you can see all the way to Skiddaw in the north and Blackpool Tower in the south. If you're not too sure of the names of all the distant peaks then head up onto the top of the Hospice, and there you'll find a wonderful old pointing device for identifying the fells and other landmarks. The steps up the side are steep and tricky to negotiate, especially in wet weather, but spare a thought for the first folks to venture up there; for many years there was no hand rail or iron railings around the top – hard to imagine in these health and safety conscious days! The railings were apparently added later by a relative of Rev. Remington, possibly in response to a comment in a prominent guide book of the time suggesting a railing was needed. Above the doorway is a Greek inscription, a quote from Homer that translates as 'rosy-fingered dawn', probably a reference to the fact that it faces directly into the sunrise and, especially on crisp winter mornings, there's no more beautiful place to start the day.

As you rejoin the road after passing through the farmland, pause for a moment and look around you. Behind you are a number of beautiful old Victorian houses and up to your right is Charney Close, where the houses are considerably younger. This is where Charney Hall School used to be – a boys school which opened in 1889 and was home to around 20 or so boarders as well as a larger number of day pupils (there are no exact records of the day students). It was situated here to

Holme Island

Limestone crags, Eden Mount

Charney Well

Settling Pools, Eggerslack Woods

View over the promenade, Grange-over-Sands

Hampsfell Hospice

ensure that the boys got plenty of fresh air, and an old advert for the school from 1967 proudly points out that school is "...350 feet above sea level". The school was extensive, with its own swimming pool and cricket pitch, and the main building was a beautiful, imposing, Victorian mansion with stunning views out across the bay. Sadly the school closed in the early 1970s and was demolished to make way for the small cul-de-sac of modern houses we see today.

Satellite strolls

Ornamental Gardens (adjacent to the railway station)

These were created in 1865 from a plot of old marshland and are a popular spot for visitors and locals. Throughout the year there are a variety of different birds to enjoy on the pond, which is fed by Picklefoot Spring (reputed never to run dry even in the longest and hottest of summers). During December the park is brightened up by one of the tallest lit Christmas trees in the country; Christmas doesn't start in Grange before the tree has been lit.

Brown Robin Nature Reserve

This is tucked away up behind the Netherwood Hotel and is more challenging than a stroll around the Ornamental Gardens. The site is owned and managed by Cumbria Wildlife Trust and there are a number of short woodland walks and some glorious views out over the estuary and the bay. If you enjoy birdwatching then this is a good spot to visit, with rare and interesting visitors throughout the year.

The promenade

The original prom in Grange is the small section running from the railway station along the edge of the Ornamental Gardens, with the rest of it having been built between 1902 and 1904 to disguise the sewage pipes. Harold Porritt, a wealthy local, funded the building of the prom, together with the tea rooms and bandstand. He also insisted that there was ramped access to the prom over the railway line, as a large number of visitors to Grange used bath chairs.

Crook Wheel
Cark
Rosthwaite
Flookburgh
A
Sand Gate
Wain Gate
Holes Farm
Mire Side
Mire Side Farm
Ravenstown
Strand Br
Lenibrick Point
Cut Bridge
Ducky's Park Farm
Winder Br
Canon Winder
Raven Winder
West Plain Farm
B
Cowpren Point
Gully Nab
Cross Bank

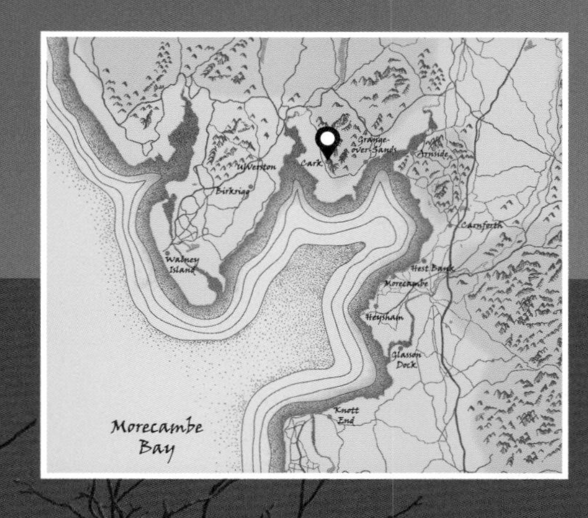

Cark

Route details

Start: The Engine Inn, Cark

Grid Ref: SD 36311 76494

Distance: 4.8 miles/7.7km

Terrain: Tarmac, hard track, stone beach

Difficulty: A mostly flat walk across a variety of different terrains. **It is advisable to check tide times before setting out as particularly high tides may affect some parts of this route**

Parking: Free street parking in Cark – please park considerately

Public transport: Trains and local buses

Facilities: Pubs and cafés in Cark, public toilets near start of walk

Our top picks: The Engine Inn, Cark – perfect place for a pint at the start, or end, of the walk. Hope and Anchor, Flookburgh – ideal if you need an extra push to the finish

Best picnic spot: There are some nice rocks to perch on around Lenibrick Point

Overview

This route forms part of the ancient Cistercian Way and the enclosed tracks towards the start of the walk really give a feel for the history of the area. The Cistercian Way itself crossed the sands over to Ulverston, but routes across the sands should only be undertaken with an appropriate guide.

Route

As you face the Engine Inn take the road leading down the left-hand side of the pub and continue on, following the lane as it crosses the stream, until you reach a railway crossing. Cross the railway and follow the hard track around the coast. Continue following this coastal path all the way around the headland, finishing with a long stretch along the top of an embankment leading to the Lakes Holiday Village (**Point B**). Take the straight road (Moor Lane) leading away from the coast and continue on into Flookburgh. In the centre of the village bear left then immediately right to follow Station Road and remain on this road back to Cark.

ESCAPE ROUTE: When you reach a small car park near the farm (**Point A**) turn left along the tarmac lane. Just beyond the farm look for the enclosed public footpath leading off to the left. Follow this (ignoring other signs to Cark) all the way up and over the railway bridge. When you drop down the far side turn left to return to the start point (1.9 miles).

About the walk

One of the things I love about this route is that it's nice and easy to follow; just a few navigational points and other than that, plenty of time to relax and enjoy the views. As with all good routes it starts at a pub – the Engine Inn, a lovely old seventeenth-century coaching inn with cosy indoor seating in the winter and plenty of sunny seats outside in the summer.

As I've mentioned in other walks, routes around the bay were rare historically, as much of the land surrounding the bay was boggy and impassable. In 1796, the Cartmel Enclosure Act provided for the construction of 24 public highways around this region. 79 additional 'private carriageways' were also constructed and together these were a dramatic improvement on what had existed before. J. Stockdale in *Annals of Cartmel* (1870) noted that "...there were formed and made many excellent roads, covered throughout with small broken stones in the place of ruinous old clog-wheel cart and pack horse tracks; many wide and useful bridges built where previously there were merely unsafe fords and slippery stepping stones." We barely give a thought to transportation now and find it hard to imagine what life must have been like before the car, but if you follow the enclosed lane on the escape route and pause for a moment, you can almost hear the old horses and carriages trundling along the lane behind you.

St John the Baptist church, Flookburgh

Out around the coast, Lenibrick Point marks the start, or end, of one important crossing point leading out across the sands to Chapel Island and Ulverston (Ulverston Walk) and the large boulders around there make the perfect place to rest and enjoy your picnic if you have one.

One of the surprising constant accompaniments to this walk is the sound of small aircraft. Nearby Cark Airfield these days is a busy gliding and parachuting centre but during the war it was an operational RAF base. During World War I considerable time and effort was invested into developing it as a base for building airships, to the extent that the nearby, and otherwise unexplained, settlement of Ravenstown was planned to house the workers. The town plan and street names were agreed and building work began on 27th March 1917; the streets were to be named after famous historical battles such as Somme, Arras and Jutland, and the house designs were the same as those near another airship base at Inchinnan near Glasgow.

A Vicker's employee, Sam Grundy, who oversaw the building work, kept a dairy so there is a full and detailed account of the development. Like any major build, and as anyone who has ever watched Grand Designs will expect, things went far from smoothly and problems with the weather (floods, snow, gales and a heatwave) and suppliers hampered progress. The house bricks were originally supposed to come from Barrow, but these were too expensive so bricks from Askham were used instead and the roofs were made from Coniston slate.

By the end of 1917, 120 houses had been built; the only problem was that the airship project had been cancelled in September 1917 so the houses were no longer required to house the airship workers. Despite that, during 1918/19 the estate filled up and was well catered for, with its own doctor's surgery and newsagents.

The old airship base was taken over by the RAF in 1941 and operated as a fighter station to protect north-west England, which was home to much of the country's heavy industry. As the war progressed the site became a training station and, following the end of the war, the station wound down and was eventually closed in May 1947. If you're following this walk on a clear, still day expect to see plenty of aircraft coming and going as folks take on the challenge of parachute jumping; some are professionals and keen amateur enthusiasts, but many are first-timers raising money for good causes.

The Haven Holiday park, as you turn to head back inland, is situated on a site which carriers fond, but mixed, memories for locals. Steve grew up nearby and remembers it as The Ponderosa, a local indoor pool where school swimming lessons took place, with a painful rough concrete floor and a pervasive smell of chlorine. There was also a vibrant Flookburgh Formula 5 racing club which used to meet and race around a small circuit there. Sadly it is now all buried under the new campsite development – but there is a nice bar there if you need a rest at this point in the walk.

Further along the road is a bit of rather more recent history, in the form of the Cartmel Sticky Toffee Pudding Company factory. The enterprise began in Cartmel over 20 years ago with puddings being made in the back of the shop (which is still there in the heart of the village), but the puddings tasted so good that they had to keep making more and more and soon outstripped their tiny surroundings. Today their puddings are distributed around the UK and across the globe, and who can resist a nice hot sticky toffee pudding fresh from the oven? The only debate is what to top it with: cream, ice-cream, custard or all three?

As you make your way back towards Cark there are another couple of buildings to note along the way. The first is St John the Baptist church. The church you see today was built between 1897 and 1900 but replaces a previous church which had been there since 1777. It's built from local slates and sandstone and in the nave of the church are commandment boards and the coat of arms for George III which were taken from the original building.

The other building is Wesley House on the final approach to the village, now a private home but a reminder of the visits John Wesley made to the county and the lasting impression he made. He arrived across the sands, visiting Flookburgh in 1759 and travelling extensively through the south of the county; the many Methodist churches in the region are testament to the impact of his work.

Satellite strolls

Holker Hall

Although there is an entry charge Holker Hall and gardens are famed for their historical and horticultural gems. The gardens cover over 23 acres and offer a variety of habitats to explore and the hall is open to visitors, with a range of festivals and fairs taking place throughout the year, as well as an excellent café.

Humphrey Head

Famously this is reputedly the site where the last wolf in England was killed (a sumptuous local ale from Unsworth's in nearby Cartmel is named Last Wolf to commemorate this). It's a limestone headland with a moderate climb but offering far-reaching views across the bay – I'm particularly fond of the furthermost point and its sense of wonderful isolation.

Bigland Hill and Tarn

A bit of a steeper walk but there are a variety of paths through ancient woodlands up to the tarn. Being wooded there's not much in the way of distant views but it is a pretty and interesting walk which is less popular than most, so ideal if you're after a bit of peace and quiet.

Oath Spring
B
Town Bank
Ulverston
Moss Nook
Brockhole Spring
Next Ness Farm
Plumpton
Oubis Hill
A
Rame Hill
Lundy Hall
Canal Foot
South Ulverston
Dragley Beck

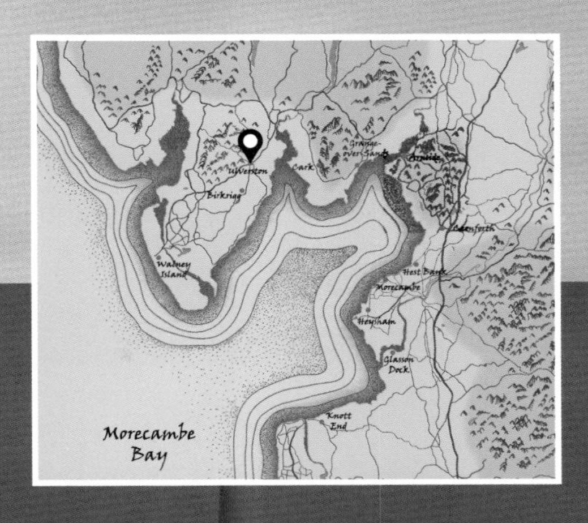

Ulverston

Route details

Start: Canal Foot car park

Grid Ref: SD 31327 77660

Distance: 4.5 miles/7.2km

Terrain: Tarmac, hard track

Difficulty: One sharp hill, but other than that flat or downhill

Parking: Free car parking at Canal Foot

Public transport: Local buses and trains in Ulverston, nothing directly to Canal Foot

Facilities: Pub at start of route, other facilities along the route

Our top picks: The Stan Laurel Inn – just off the route but definitely worth finding. They stock a popular gin brewed nearby in a tiny garden shed (and appropriately named Shed 1). The Bay Horse – lovely pub and chock full of local history too

Best picnic spot: Either the benches around Canal Foot or up on Hoad Hill

The Hoad (or Sir John Barrow Monument), Ulverston

Overview

Ulverston is a town full of interesting corners to explore and once you've completed this route it's definitely worth taking a look at the satellite strolls, or just taking a gentle amble around the town. The canal is a haven for wildlife as well as playing a crucial role in Ulverston's past, and The Hoad is the perfect viewpoint from which to admire the town. Top tip – look for days when the flag is flying as that means The Hoad is open and you can explore right to the very top.

Route

From the car park at Canal Foot follow the canal all the way up to the road at the top (turn right here to locate Booths with café and toilets). Turn left and cross the road, following it towards the town, then keep right as the footpath forks away from the road and up along Sunderland Terrace. When you join another road keep right then turn right along Poplar Grove (**Point A**). Continue on this small road as it narrows to a path and climbs gradually to meet a lane at the foot of Hoad Hill. Cross the lane and enter Hoad Hill Park via the large kissing gate.

Follow the tarmac track as it winds up to The Hoad (there are a number of alternative routes of varying steepness if you're feeling fit!). After visiting the monument take the broad gravel track leading away from the town and remain on it as it winds down and around the fields behind the hill. After half a mile follow the wall as it drops away to your left leading to a metal kissing gate (**Point B).** Pass through the gate and follow the enclosed path downhill. Continue straight on, passing through several kissing gates and crossing a couple of small residential lanes until you reach a T-junction.

Turn left here and follow the lane for a short distance until it emerges in front of a hospice. Turn right to follow the road down to the entrance to Ford Park, then turn right and then left to follow a small alleyway on to Hart Street. Turn left here to return to Sunderland Terrace then retrace your steps back to the canal and the start of the walk.

ESCAPE ROUTE: Simply walk along the canal and back and save Hoad Hill for another day (2.5 miles).

About the walk

Ulverston isn't the first place many visitors think about heading to, but it has a lot to offer, in terms of views, walks and, of course, great places to eat and drink.

Before you get stuck into the walk, pause for a moment at Canal Foot to look out across Morecambe Bay and just a short distance away you'll see Chapel Island. **(NOTE: Even if it looks accessible at low tide please do NOT try to reach the island without an appropriate guide.)** Predictably, Chapel Island takes its name from the chapel on the island, although the ruins that are there today are the remains of a folly from the early nineteenth century.

Back in the times before road and rail transport made getting from A to B fairly straightforward, the most obvious way to get around Morecambe Bay was across the sands. Imagine you're looking at a map of the bay back in the early 1800s and wanted to get from Cark to Ulverston; it would make a lot more sense to set off across the bay than to walk all the way up and around via Greenodd. Back then people would

Town mural, Ulverston

Laurel and Hardy statue, Coronation Hall, Ulverston

Ulverston Canal

Leven Viaduct

have been much more in tune with the tides and the sands than we are today and 'safe' routes across the sands would have been known, well-trodden and possibly marked in some way. Of course people would still have been caught out and places like Chapel Island would have provided a refuge for those getting their timings a bit wrong.

When they got their timings right they would arrive, or depart, from the Bay Horse, a seventeenth-century coaching inn and now the perfect place for food and drink at the start (or end) of a walk. The inn highlights the significance of the town as a vital local market and the importance of this crossing point over the sands. Farmers and traders from all around the local area would arrive in the town, together with carriages of visitors, making market days busy, bustling and profitable affairs.

Ulverston Canal was completed in 1796 in order to make the town more accessible; the original estimate for building it was £3000 but it cost over £9000 by the time it was completed (the equivalent of estimating around £200,000 and coming in at well over half a million in today's money!). The canal is 1.25 miles (2km) long, 15 ft (4.6m) deep and 66ft (20m wide) and is reputed to be the straightest canal in Britain. It was built to provide access for the large boats and other vessels supporting the various heavy industries in the area and was a vital supply line until the railways arrived in the late 1800s. From then on the canal trade went into decline and it eventually closed to commercial traffic after World War II. Today it is jointly maintained by GlaxoSmithKline and the very active and enthusiastic Ulverston Canal Regeneration Group, who raise funds throughout the year to maintain the footpaths and support the wildlife along the canal.

Bay Horse Hotel and Leven Estuary

The Hoad is Ulverston's most noticeable monument and it's hard to miss (there are some great long-distance views of it from the Birkrigg Walk). Officially it is the Sir John Barrow Monument and was built to commemorate the life of the said man, who was born in the town. Sir John excelled in mathematics and his distinguished career took him to the rank of Second Secretary to the Admiralty, where he promoted British exploration, particularly around West Africa and the North Polar Region, and he was heavily involved in attempts to discover the North West Passage through the Canadian Arctic. In 1830 he was a founder member of the Royal Geographical Society and played a key role in the society's development until his death in 1834. The Hoad itself (known locally as The Pepperpot) is 100ft high and built from limestone quarried from Birkrigg. The 112 narrow, winding stairs leading to the top of the tower are not for the faint hearted, but those braving the climb will be rewarded with superb views across the Lakeland fells to the north and Morecambe Bay to the south.

Ulverston's other, and arguably more famous, son is Stan Laurel, who was born in the town in June 1890. Although he only lived there for the first six years of his life he returned to holiday there with his grandparents throughout his school years and the town made a lasting impression on him. He often mentioned the narrow, cobbled, streets in letters to friends and, as a child, he was fond of pulling faces in the large glass windows when he was taken into town on shopping trips. If you take a slight deviation from the walk to explore the town you'll find a wonderful statue of Laurel and Hardy in front of Coronation Hall and a whole museum dedicated to the duo in the nearby cinema.

Ulverston was granted its Market Charter by Edward I on 11th September 1280 during his visit to the county, and a market is still held in the town every Thursday and Saturday. Although there are numerous events in the town throughout the year one of the busiest and most popular is the Dickensian Festival which takes place in late November and transports the town back in time, with many stallholders, and visitors, dressing in period costume. There are a variety of activities for all the family, including horse-drawn carriage rides and plenty of warming festive food and drink.

Satellite strolls

Town centre

I'm not the biggest fan of town centres, but Ulverston is lovely with plenty of interesting alleyways to explore and a good selection of local shops in amongst the usual high street chains. The bottom end of Market Street is always a favourite place for me and I can't imagine it's changed much since the days Stan Laurel used to visit. There's also a lovely mural of the town's history along one of the alleyways; it's beautifully bright, colourful and informative.

Cumbria Way

This is a long-distance footpath which stretches all the way from Ulverston to Carlisle. It takes in some of the most spectacular scenery in the Lake District and is well signposted throughout the town. If you fancy stretching your legs, the first mile or so up and out of Ulverston makes for a very pleasant walk.

Outcast Ropeworks (just to the west of this walk)

We really wanted to include this as part of the walk, but couldn't manage it without significantly increasing the mileage and directing you along some fairly mundane residential roads; however it is a short and historically interesting walk. In 1752, the Outcast Ropeworks was established to support the local shipping industry and they required a long, straight area to lay out the ropes – in this case 1282 ft (390m). The area is now a 'Greenway' route with plenty of information boards along the way.

Ulverston mural

Birkrigg stone circle

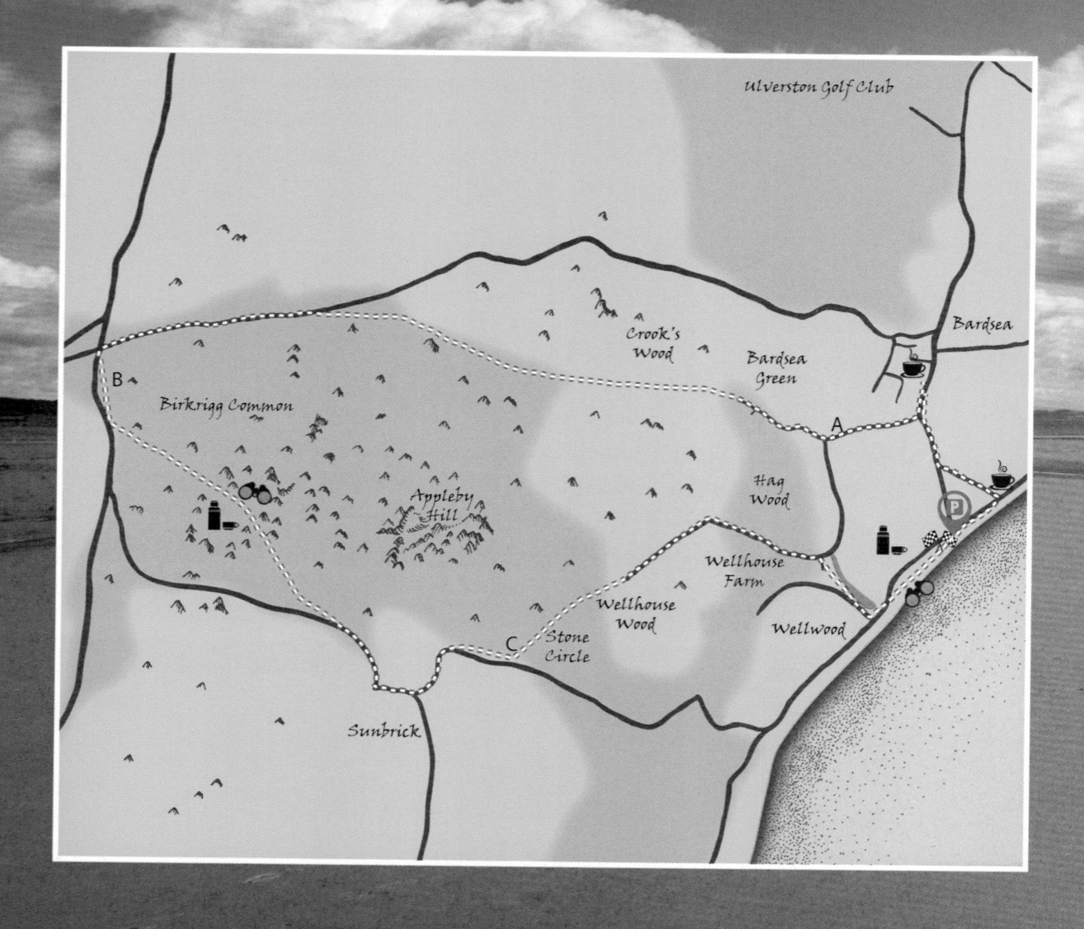

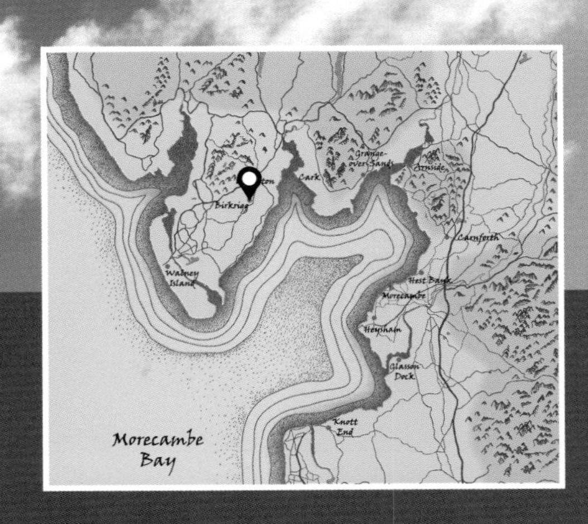

Birkrigg

Route Details

Start: Seafront car park

Grid Ref: SD 30299 74348

Distance: 3.5 miles/5.6km

Terrain: Tarmac, hard track, grass

Difficulty: A couple of short hills but other than that a gentle and relaxing walk

Parking: Free car parking along the seafront at Bardsea

Public transport: Local buses

Facilities: Café at start and pub along route

Our top picks: Roy's ice cream van (always in the car park) because every walk deserves an ice cream! The Ship Inn, Bardsea – a lovely, friendly, proper local pub

Best picnic spot: Either the benches along the coast at the start/end of the walk or the bench near the trig point

Overview

The two short hills towards the start of this walk are more than compensated for by the views; it's hard to think of a single section of this walk which doesn't have a lovely view. From Birkrigg Common there are 360 degree views to the fells, The Hoad in Ulverston and, of course, Morecambe Bay, which looks particularly beautiful at low tide with a myriad channels criss-crossing the bay.

Route

From the car park walk up the short, steep street leading away from the shore (Main Street). At the top turn right towards Bardsea; when you reach the first road junction continue on to the right to visit the church and pub, then return and follow the small lane downhill towards Bardsea Green and Well House (**Point A**). At the bottom of the lane, where the road forks, bear right towards Bardsea Green and remain on this road as it climbs steadily, passing a number of driveways, and continue on as it becomes a broad grassy track, narrowing as it climbs towards a wooden gate.

Pass through the gate and follow the grassy path leading directly away from the gate. Remain on this wide track until it drops to the right to reach a tarmac road. Bear left and follow the broad grassy verge along the road to the junction then turn left towards Scales (**Point B).** After 100m, at the end of the small crags, turn left to follow a broad grassy path up towards the top of the common; near the top bear right to reach the trig point.

From the trig point continue on towards the coast, following another broad grassy track down to join a small tarmac road. Bear left along this and follow it as it winds down around a cluster of farmhouses. After a sharp right-hand bend the road straightens and continues downhill, bear left after 50m to follow a broad track leading out across the common (**Point C**). Remain on this track, passing the stone circle on your right, until you reach a metal gate. Pass through the gate and continue down until you reach a cluster of houses. Take the signed footpath to the shore on your right and follow this path back to the shoreline. Once you reach the shore, turn left to return to the starting point.

ESCAPE ROUTE: At **Point A** turn left to follow the lane towards Well House Farm (**Point C**), and from here follow the signed route back to the shoreline, then turn left to follow the shore back to the starting point (1 mile).

About the walk

Birkrigg Common is an excellent place to get lost, figuratively rather than literally. There are dozens of criss-crossing paths, each of which offers new and exciting views of Morecambe Bay and the surrounding hills so, if you have a map, don't be afraid to branch out away from the walk and indulge in a little off-piste exploration.

Towards the start of the walk is Holy Trinity Church in Bardsea (not far from the pub!); the views from the front of the church are glorious and there are a few interesting features inside too. The church was designed by local architect George Webster in 1843. The Webster

Bardsea Monument

Swarthmoor Hall

family were a prominent family of architects who were responsible for many of the buildings around the county at the end of the nineteenth century, including the façade of Kendal Town Hall and what is now the HSBC bank in the middle of the town. Before the church was built people worshipped in the nearby schoolrooms, but on October 20th 1843 the foundation stone for Holy Trinity was laid. Unfortunately the building of the rest of the church was delayed when the original funder was declared bankrupt. Eventually a local gentleman, Thomas Petty, offered a considerable donation and raised the rest by public subscription. The church was eventually completed in 1854.

The stained glass windows in the apse were designed by Wilhelmina Geddes, an important figure in the Arts and Crafts movement in the early twentieth century, and show Christ emerging from the tomb. In 1998 the church underwent a complete refurbishment, funded by what is reputed to be the first ever Heritage Lottery Fund grant.

As you leave the village you'll pass the Malt Kiln on your right. This, as the name suggests, is where they once roasted malt for brewing and dates back to 1829. Following World War II, a local family bought the hall and set up a trust as a memorial to those who lost their lives; today it serves as the village hall and is a hub of activity for recreational events and local celebrations.

Stained glass windows, Holy Trinity Church, Bardsea

Hoad hill and Sir John Barrow Monument

Birkrigg Stone circle

As you get up onto Birkrigg Common there are excellent views over the Lake District fells, as well as rather lovely views of The Hoad above Ulverston (see Ulverston Walk). A little closer in, in the middle of the nearby golf course, is Bardsea Monument. Made from local limestone the monument was built in 1830 as a mausoleum for the local Gale family and stands in what were once the grounds of Bardsea Hall. The architect was Thomas Richard Gale-Braddyll, who came from a wealthy and influential local family; when his father died in 1818 Thomas inherited a lot of local land, including nearby Conishead Priory which he extended from what was described at the time as a "gentlemen's house" into the glorious Gothic structure we see today. Unfortunately he was the same gentlemen who had initially funded Holy Trinity Church and when he lost all his money he was forced to sell Conishead Priory, still not quite completed, in 1851.

Sadly Bardsea Hall, having passed through the hands of several different owners, is now long gone and all that remains is the monument. Its unusual triangular form is said to face the directions from which the original three branches of the family hailed: the Wilsons of Bardsea, the Braddylls of Conishead Priory and the Gales of Whitehaven (whose ancestors fought in the American War of Independence).

The stone circle up on Birkrigg Common is notable for being one of the very few double stone circles in the UK and the only one in Cumbria. There is an inner ring of 10 to 12 stones and an outer ring of 15 to 20 (counting stones in stone circles is notoriously tricky and is often shrouded in local folklore). All of the stones are local limestone and the circles date back to the Bronze Age, 1700–1400 years ago.

For many years, only the inner circle was visible but a considerable amount of work has been done recently, driven by Morecambe Bay Partnership and carried out by a tireless team of volunteers, to reveal the outer circle. The existence of the outer circle came as a surprise to many locals as it had been hidden by bracken for decades, but regular 'bracken bashing' work parties have cleared the site and revealed it in all its glory. From excavations carried out in the early twentieth century it is thought that the stone circle had ceremonial significance, as a pestle and mortar and fragments of ochre dye were found at the site.

I still feel as if I've only scratched the surface with Bardsea and Birkrigg; for such small places they punch well above their weight when it comes to interesting and influential history. In addition to what I've already mentioned Bardsea was an important port for Roman trading, was mentioned in the Doomsday book (as Barretsiege), was home to local influential families involved in the setting up of Furness Abbey as well as Conishead Priory, and the land which is now the golf course and was once Bardsea Hall was, before all of that and even before the local Abbey and Priory were established, occupied by a hospital of St John of Jerusalem, possibly dating back as far as 1202. Bardsea is proof that you don't have to be big to be impressive.

Satellite strolls

Conishead Priory

There is a great café here and a number of excellent gentle strolls around the extensive gardens, leading all the way down to the shoreline with its superb view across to Chapel Island. You can also find the remains of an old railway line which once cut through here, dating back to a time when the priory was a hydropathic hotel and popular enough to merit its own branch line.

Great Urswick & Urswick Tarn

The nearby village of Great Urswick is worth a visit for a stroll around the tarn. There's a bench where you can sit and enjoy a picnic, or a local pub to retreat into if you prefer. If you fancy stretching your legs look on the OS Map for the route leading north past the remains of the fort – there are some more lovely views from up there on a clear day.

Dalton-in-Furness

Dalton is an interesting and much overlooked little town which has a few interesting bits and pieces, not least of which is the castle at the top of the town which dates back to the fourteenth century. There's also a pleasant circular walk over past the church and down along Poaka Beck – or you could continue on all the way to Furness Abbey if you're feeling fit!

Ulverston and Hoad Hill

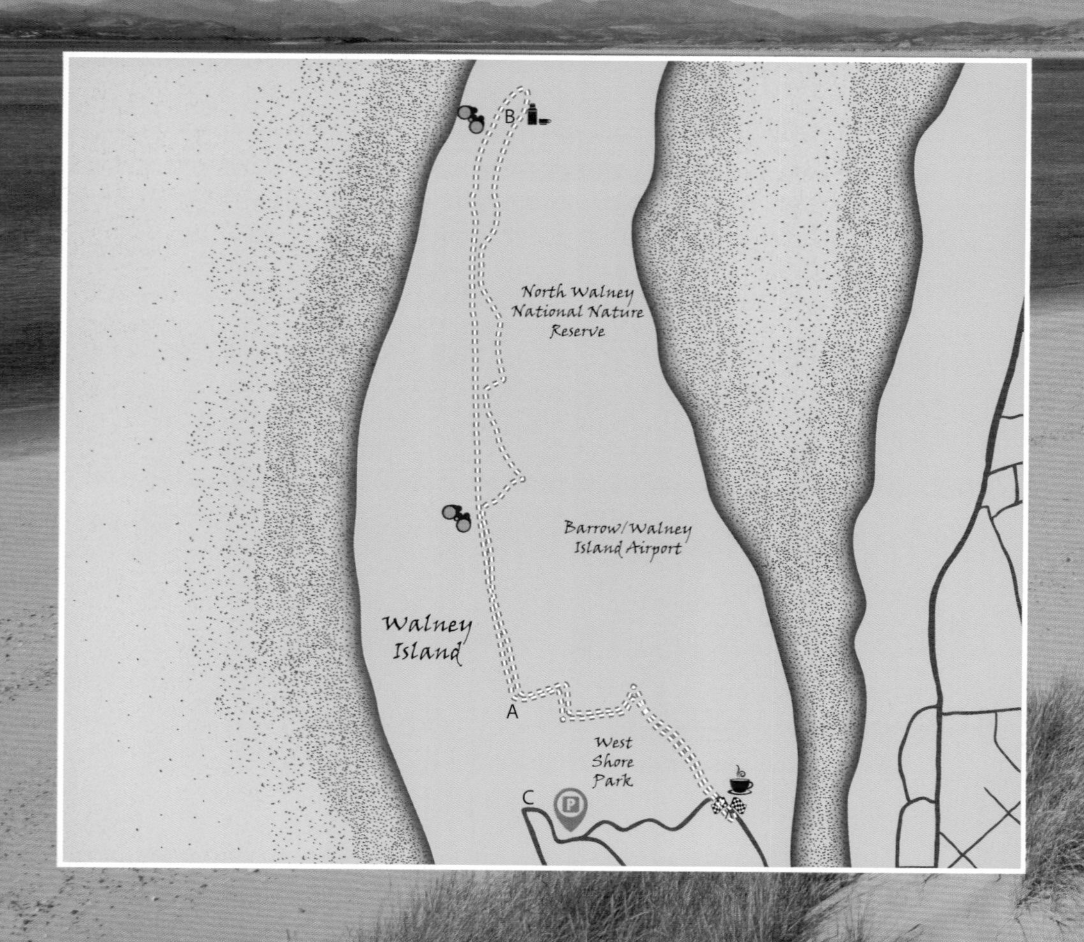
B
North Walney
National Nature
Reserve
Barrow/Walney
Island Airport
Walney
Island
A
West
Shore
Park
C

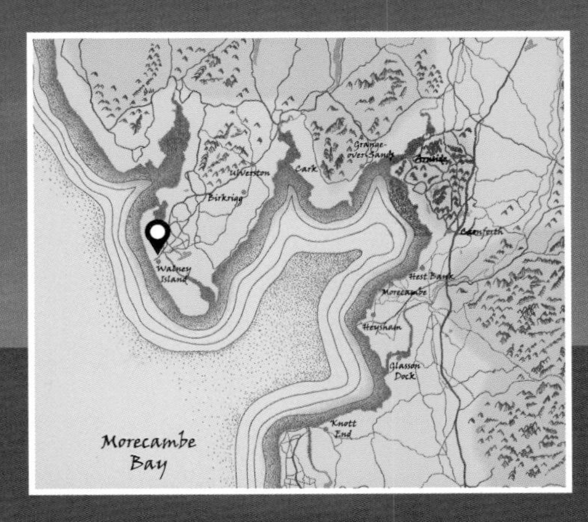

Walney Island

Route details

Start: Crown Pub, North Scale

Grid Ref: SD 18189 69961

Distance: 5 miles/8km

Terrain: Tarmac, hard track, sand

Difficulty: A straightforward walk with ample opportunity to extend your exploration among the sand dunes

Parking: Limited on-road parking near pub. Alternative start: begin the walk at the car park on the seafront adjacent to West Shore Park (**Point C**) at grid ref: SD 17089 69933 – the pub is a three-minute drive from this point

Public Transport: Regular buses from Barrow

Facilities: Crown Pub at start of walk

Our top picks: The Crown Pub – the only pub on the route but newly refurbished with good beer and generous portions of food. Andy's Fish & Chips, Vickerstown (not on the map) – go grab a bag of greasy goodness and watch the sunset from the beach, just a short drive away

Best picnic spot: Anywhere along the sand dunes, although the dunes at the far north are quieter and have the best views

Black Combe and Duddon Estuary

Overview

This is a popular spot with locals and is perfect during the summer for a quick dip at high tide. The sand dunes are extensive and the views to the north and Black Combe are glorious. Beware if you visit in winter or poor weather as Walney is notoriously exposed and bears the brunt of onshore winds.

Route

With the pub on your right walk along the road and continue as it narrows until you reach the entrance to the airport. Turn left here to follow the permissive path to the shore (**Point A**). At the shore turn right and remain on the broad hard track towards the dunes. Continue on as it narrows to a light-coloured gravel, single-track path along the top of the dunes. Follow this path as it bears right and then left along the airport perimeter fence.

Enter the nature reserve through the kissing gate and remain on the broad track as it winds through the reserve. Immediately after the large green metal gate covered with bird statues, keep to the left fork to remain on this track to the kissing gate at the northern end of the reserve. Pass through this gate and fork left again to continue on the broad track until it peters out in the dunes.

At this point there are a number of small paths and 'sheep trods' criss-crossing the dunes. Using these paths continue heading north (towards Black Combe, the large fell in the distance) until you reach the shoreline (**Point B**). At the shore turn left to follow the sea shore back to **Point A** then turn left onto the permissive path to retrace your steps back to the pub.

ESCAPE ROUTE: At any point return to the shoreline, turn left, return to **Point A**, and retrace steps to the pub.

About the walk

Although this is the most limited of all the walks in terms of the number of pub (or grub) places on offer, we really wanted to include it, as north Walney is such a wonderful and unexpected place to explore. As you'll see from the photographs on a sunny day you could almost be in the Caribbean, except for beautiful Black Combe that looms large to the north, and you know there will be an excellent pint and a decent pie and chips at the end.

If the weather isn't so great then an afternoon at the Dock Museum in Barrow is the perfect way to warm up and pass the time, and the ideal way to learn more about the history of both Barrow and the fabulous Walney Island (it also has a great café!).

There is evidence to suggest that people have lived and hunted on Walney since at least 5000BCE. The ice sheet retreated from the area around 13,000 years ago and there's evidence of hunter gatherers elsewhere in the county going back to 12,000 years ago. A relic of the ice age is the submerged forest off the coast of Walney which is revealed only during very low tides. When the ice sheets were around, sea levels

were lower and forests once flourished around our shores, but these became submerged as the ice melted and the sea rose once again.

There is very little evidence of Romans on the island, just a couple of small finds of a few coins and a bracelet, but it's possible that they used the island as a trading post. The island was also once part of the land owned by Furness Abbey, with the monks raising rabbits on the island for meat and working with the locals to repair and maintain sea walls and dykes. Most notably, Biggar Dyke was built by the abbey to protect North Scale and Biggar and the locals were required to maintain it as part of their tithe to the abbey. After the abbey was dissolved in 1537 the dyke fell into disrepair and was breached by storms. Following a hearing at the Duchy Court in Lancaster it was agreed that rents in the two villages would be reduced so long as the villagers continued to repair the dyke (although each village was convinced that they did more than their fair share and the other village were a bunch of slackers!).

Many people are surprised to find an active airfield on the island. It was completed in 1941 after the compulsory purchase of North End Farm, which had previously occupied the land. At that time the volume of grain production on the island was such that two separate mills were required, one of which stood at North End Farm. The mill ceased production in 1870 but was not demolished until the airfield was being built during 1940, and it's rumoured that the old millstones were broken up and used within the runway foundations.

During World War II over 5000 RAF students received training at the airfield. After Cark airfield (see Ulverston Walk) closed in early 1946 the local Mountain Rescue unit moved here until the airport finally closed later that same year. The site remained in government hands until it was bought by Vickers (now BAe systems) in 1959, who still own the land. Commercial flights operated during the 1980s and 1990s but these days, despite several different plans being proposed in the past and more recently, the airport only operates private flights.

The views to the north are dominated by Black Combe, which is formed from the Skiddaw Group of rocks, some of oldest in Cumbria. It was formed during the Ordovician era around 460 million years ago and was visibly shaped by the glaciers many millennia later. It is listed as one of Wainwright's 'Outlying Fells' and because it's not in his main list of fells is generally much quieter, even on a sunny bank holiday. I think the views from the top are hard to beat, but don't just take my word for it, William Wordsworth himself waxed lyrical:

> For from the summit of Black Comb (dread name
> Derived from clouds and storms!) the amplest range
> Of unobstructed prospect may be seen

The beaches and dunes of North Walney

Of course all of that was said before the offshore windfarm was built, which remains controversial, and I'm pretty sure Mr Wordsworth would not have approved of it! It is currently the world's largest wind farm, covering an area of 55 square miles, and it generates enough energy to power over 600,000 homes. The first turbine was built in 2011 and today there are 189, and although it generates an impressive amount of energy, and provides local employment, from a conservation and aesthetics stand point it sharply divides opinion. The Irish Sea is a haven for wildlife and the wind farm borders one of two local Marine Conservation Zones, which are basically nature reserves in the sea which are protected from development because of their rare or threatened habitats.

One of the constant battles Walney has fought over the centuries is that of erosion. It juts out into the Irish Sea and regularly takes a battering when the winter storms come in, and following extensive erosion caused by Storm Desmond in December 2015, parts of South Walney are regularly cut off at high tides. West Shore Park (caravans), next to the alternative start point for this walk, is very badly affected by storms and the western edges are particularly vulnerable, so significant funding is currently being sought to improve sea defences around the entire island.

Satellite strolls

South Walney Nature Reserve

This nature reserve is owned and managed by Cumbria Wildlife Trust and there is a small honesty box for car park charges. As well as a variety of bird hides and laid-out paths around the reserve, there is also an interesting cabin full of strange and unusual finds from the local beaches around the reserve.

Foulney Island

I am very fond of a walk out onto nearby Foulney Island – it gets cut off during high tides and the last time we visited we spent a blissful couple of hours stranded out there in the sunshine enjoying a picnic – although you may not have the time for this, so do check the tide times! Do take note of warning signs to protect ground nesting birds during the spring/summer.

Roa Island

This is another small local island with a fascinating history. Until 1847 it was a true island but then the causeway was built providing a permanent access to the mainland. There's a great café there and a couple of interesting buildings, especially the old Customs House on the east of the island. You can also take a short ferry ride from there over to Piel Island and discover yet more fabulous local history.

Black Combe